RICE COOKER

Quarto.com

© 2025 Quarto Publishing Group USA Inc.
Text © 2012 Beth Hensperger and Julie Kaufmann

First Published in 2025 by The Harvard Common Press, an imprint of The Quarto Group,
100 Cummings Center, Suite 265-D, Beverly, MA 01915, USA.
T (978) 282-9590 F (978) 283-2742

The Harvard Common Press titles are also available at discount for retail, wholesale, promotional, and bulk purchase. For details, contact the Special Sales Manager by email at specialsales@quarto.com or by mail at The Quarto Group, Attn: Special Sales Manager, 100 Cummings Center, Suite 265-D, Beverly, MA 01915, USA.

29 28 27 26 25   1 2 3 4 5

ISBN: 978-0-7603-9741-1

Digital edition published in 2025
eISBN: 978-0-7603-9742-8

Library of Congress Cataloging-in-Publication Data
Names: Harvard Common Press, editor.
Title: Rice cooker / editors of the Harvard Common Press.
Description: Beverly, MA, USA : The Harvard Common Press, an imprint of The
    Quarto Group, 2025. | Series: The time-pressed cook | Includes
    bibliographical references and index.
Identifiers: LCCN 2024054175 | ISBN 9780760397411 (hardcover) | ISBN
    9780760397428 (ebook)
Subjects: LCSH: Electric cooking. | Electric rice cookers. | Cooking
    (Rice). | LCGFT: Cookbooks.
Classification: LCC TX827 .R53 2025 | DDC 641.6/318--dc23/eng/20241205
LC record available at https://lccn.loc.gov/2024054175

The content in this book was previously published in *The Ultimate Rice Cooker Cookbook* by Beth Hensperger (Harvard Common Press, 2012) and *The Best of the Best Rice Cooker Cookbook* by Beth Hensperger (Harvard Common Press, 2019).

Design and Page Layout: Megan Jones Design
Photography: Ellen Callaway except Shutterstock on pages 10, 12, 13, 14, 19, 23, 24, 32, 36, 39, 42, 44, 47, 51, 52, 55, 56, 60, 63, 64, 68, 71, 72, 75, 76, 78, 85, 90, 94, 97, 98, 101, 103, 105, 108, 111, 112, 115, and 120
Illustration: Michael Korfhage

Printed in China

RICE COOKER

EDITORS OF THE HARVARD COMMON PRESS

HARVARD
COMMON
PRESS

CONTENTS

Introduction: Rice Cooker Basics 6
The Perfect Pot of Rice 7

1
BREAKFASTS
11

2
EVERYDAY RICE
29

3
BEANS, LEGUMES, AND VEGETABLES
45

4

POLENTA, GRITS, AND HOMINY

61

5

PILAFS AND RISOTTOS

79

6

STEAMED DINNERS

95

7

DESSERTS

109

Index 124

INTRODUCTION:
RICE COOKER BASICS

Congratulations on your purchase of a rice cooker! It's versatile and reliable, a very nifty little bit of technology. It can make perfect rice and, as you are about to find out, much more.

Rice cookers come in standard sizes: the 3- or 4-cup [495 to 660 g] capacity (small), 5- or 6-cup [825 to 990 g] (medium), and 8- or 10- or 14-cup [1.3 or 1.7 or 2.3 kg] (large) models. Many manufacturers have models that can hold up to 20 cups for home use. The jumbo rice cooker, or deluxe cooker, has a capacity of 15 to 30 cups (2.5 to 5 kg).

There are two categories of rice cookers available on the market today: on/off and fuzzy logic. The two most basic types of on/off rice cookers are the cook-and-shut-off cooker and the cook-and-reduce-heat cooker/warmer. Each has a round metal housing with a removable aluminum rice bowl; the carrying handles are on the outer housing and there is a switch on the front of the machine. This on/off mechanism, while seemingly simple compared to the newer fuzzy logic machines, contains the same type of efficient heating elements without the digital options. In addition to making rice, it is a superior machine for steaming purposes. The cook-and-reduce heat cooker/warmer models can keep rice hot and ready to eat for several hours. The third type of on/off rice cooker is the deluxe electronic model, which is fitted with an electronic sensor unit and retains the round housing style of the other on/off cookers.

Fuzzy logic rice cookers—the basic fuzzy logic and the newer induction heating and pressure cooking machines—are immediately recognizable by their digital face, multiple-choice function buttons, and elongated housing shape. These machines are not usually set up for steaming.

THE PERFECT POT OF RICE

Follow this guide for a basic pot of rice.

RICE	MACHINE	CYCLE	YIELD	INGREDIENTS	NOTES
American Long-Grain White Rice	Medium (6-cup [990 g]) rice cooker; fuzzy logic or on/off	Regular	Serves 3 to 4	1 cup (190 g) long-grain white rice 1½ cups (355 ml) water ¼ teaspoon salt	When the machine switches to the Keep Warm cycle, let the rice steam for 10 minutes. Fluff the rice with a wooden or plastic rice paddle or wooden spoon. This rice will hold on Keep Warm for hours. Before serving, stir in 1 to 2 tablespoons (14 to 28 g) unsalted butter, margarine, olive oil, or nut oil, if desired.
Chinese-Style Plain Rice	Medium (6-cup [990 g]) rice cooker; fuzzy logic or on/off	Regular	Serves 3 to 4	1 cup (190 g) long-grain white rice 1¼ cups (295 ml) water	Rinse the rice first. Coat the rice cooker bowl with nonstick cooking spray or a film of vegetable oil. When the machine switches to the Keep Warm cycle, let the rice steam for 15 minutes. Fluff the rice with a wooden or plastic rice paddle or wooden spoon.
Basmati Rice	Medium (6-cup [990 g]) rice cooker; fuzzy logic or on/off	Regular	Serves 4	1 cup (190 g) basmati rice 1½ cups (355 ml) water ¼ teaspoon fine sea salt	Rinse the rice 2 to 4 times. When the machine switches to the Keep Warm cycle, let the rice steam for 10 minutes. Fluff the rice with a wooden or plastic rice paddle or wooden spoon.
American Jasmine Rice	Medium (6-cup [990 g]) rice cooker; fuzzy logic or on/off	Regular	Serves 6 to 8	2 cups (380 g) domestic white jasmine rice 3 cups (705 ml) water Large pinch of fine sea salt (optional)	Coat the rice cooker bowl with nonstick cooking spray or a film of vegetable oil. When the machine switches to the Keep Warm cycle, let the rice steam for 15 minutes. Fluff the rice with a wooden or plastic rice paddle or wooden spoon.
Thai Jasmine Rice	Medium (6-cup [990 g]) rice cooker; fuzzy logic or on/off	Regular	Serves 6 to 8	2 cups (380 g) Thai jasmine rice 2¼ cups (530 ml) water ¼ teaspoon salt	Rinse the rice first. Coat the rice cooker bowl with nonstick cooking spray or a film of vegetable oil. When the machine switches to the Keep Warm cycle, let the rice steam for 15 minutes. Fluff the rice with a wooden or plastic rice paddle or wooden spoon.
White Jasmine Blend	Medium (6-cup [990 g]) rice cooker; fuzzy logic or on/off	Regular	Serves 3 to 4	½ cup (90 g) long-grain white rice ½ cup (90 g) Thai jasmine rice 1½ cups (355 ml) water ¼ teaspoon salt	Rinse the rice first. Coat the rice cooker bowl with nonstick cooking spray or a film of vegetable oil. When the machine switches to the Keep Warm cycle, let the rice steam for 10 to 15 minutes. Fluff the rice with a wooden or plastic rice paddle or wooden spoon.

RICE	MACHINE	CYCLE	YIELD	INGREDIENTS	NOTES
Medium-Grain White Rice	Medium (6-cup [990 g]) rice cooker; fuzzy logic or on/off	Regular	Serves 3 to 4	1 cup (190 g) medium-grain white rice 1⅓ cups (315 ml) water ¼ teaspoon salt (optional)	Wash the rice first. When the machine switches to the Keep Warm cycle, let the rice steam for 15 minutes. Gently but thoroughly fluff the rice with a plastic or wooden rice paddle or wooden spoon.
Riso (Arborio, Carnaroli, or vialone nano rice)	Medium (6-cup [990 g]) rice cooker; fuzzy logic or on/off	Regular	Serves 4 (about 3½ cups [578 g])	1¼ cups (237.5 g) Arborio, Carnaroli, or vialone nano rice 1¾ cups (410 ml) water 1 tablespoon (15 ml) olive oil Small pinch of salt	When the machine switches to the Keep Warm cycle, let the rice steam for 10 minutes. Fluff the rice gently with a wooden or plastic rice paddle or wooden spoon.
Short-Grain White Rice	Medium (6-cup [990 g]) rice cooker; fuzzy logic or on/off	Regular	Serves 3 to 4	1½ cups (285 g) (2 rice cooker cups) short-grain white rice 1⅔ cups (395 ml) cold water ¼ teaspoon salt (optional)	Wash the rice first. Let the rice soak for 30 to 60 minutes. When the machine switches to the Keep Warm cycle, gently but thoroughly fluff the rice with a wooden or plastic rice paddle or wooden spoon. Let the rice steam for 10 to 15 minutes.
Long- or Medium-Grain Brown Rice	Medium (6-cup [990 g]) rice cooker; fuzzy logic or on/off	Regular	Serves 4	1 cup (190 g) domestic long-grain brown rice 2 cups plus 1 tablespoon (485 ml) water	Rince the rice first. When the machine switches to the Keep Warm cycle, let the rice steam for 10 to 15 minutes. Fluff the rice with a wooden or plastic rice paddle or wooden spoon.
Small-Batch Basmati Brown Rice	Small (3-cup [570 g]) or medium (6-cup [990 g]) rice cooker; fuzzy logic or on/off	Regular	Serves 1 or 2	½ cup (95 g) medium- or long-grain brown or red rice 1 cup (235 ml) water ⅛ teaspoon fine sea salt 2 teaspoons butter (optional)	Rinse the rice first. When the machine switches to the Keep Warm cycle, fluff the rice with a wooden or plastic rice paddle or wooden spoon. Cover with a paper towel, close the lid, and let the rice steam for 10 minutes to absorb the extra moisture before serving.
Short-Grain Brown Rice	Medium (6-cup [990 g]) rice cooker; fuzzy logic or on/off	Brown Rice or Regular	Serves 4	1 cup (190 g) short-grain brown rice 2¼ cups (530 ml) cold water	Rinse the rice first. When the machine switches to the Keep Warm cycle, let the rice steam for 10 to 15 minutes. Fluff the rice with a wooden or plastic rice paddle or wooden spoon.

RICE	MACHINE	CYCLE	YIELD	INGREDIENTS	NOTES
Brown Basmati Rice	Medium (6-cup [990 g]) rice cooker; fuzzy logic or on/off	Regular	Serves 4	1 cup (190 g) imported Indian brown basmati rice 2 cups (470 ml) water 1 tablespoon (14 g) unsalted butter ¼ teaspoon salt	Rinse the rice first. Coat the rice cooker bowl with nonstick cooking spray or a film of vegetable oil. When the machine switches to the Keep Warm cycle, let the rice steam for 10 minutes. Fluff the rice with a wooden or plastic rice paddle or wooden spoon.
Brown Jasmine Rice	Medium (6-cup [990 g]) rice cooker; fuzzy logic or on/off	Regular	Serves 4	1 cup (190 g) domestic brown jasmine rice 2 cups (470 ml) water 1 tablespoon (14 g) unsalted butter	Coat the rice cooker bowl with nonstick cooking spray or a film of vegetable oil. When the machine switches to the Keep Warm cycle, let the rice steam for 15 minutes. Fluff the rice with a wooden or plastic rice paddle or wooden spoon.
Wild Pecan Rice	Medium (6-cup [990 g]) rice cooker; fuzzy logic or on/off	Brown Rice or Regular	Serves 4	One 7-ounce (198 g) package Wild Pecan rice 1¾ cups (410 ml) water 2 tablespoons (28 g) unsalted butter 1 teaspoon salt	Coat the rice cooker bowl with nonstick cooking spray or a film of vegetable oil. Reserve 1 tablespoon (14 g) butter to nestle on top of the rice when serving. When the machine switches to the Keep Warm cycle, let the rice steam for 10 minutes. Fluff the rice with a wooden or plastic rice paddle or wooden spoon.
Black Rice	Medium (6-cup [990 g]) rice cooker; fuzzy logic or on/off	Brown Rice or Regular	Serves 4	1 cup (190 g) Forbidden Rice (Chinese black rice) 1¾ cups (410 ml) water ¼ teaspoon salt (optional)	Rinse the rice first. Coat the rice cooker bowl with nonstick cooking spray or a film of vegetable oil. When the machine switches to the Keep Warm cycle, open and dry the inside of the cover. Crumple a clean paper towel and place it over the rice to absorb excess moisture. Close the cover and let the rice steam for 15 minutes. Remove the paper towel. Fluff the rice with a wooden or plastic rice paddle or wooden spoon.
Black Japonica Rice	Medium (6-cup [990 g]) rice cooker; fuzzy logic or on/off	Brown Rice or Regular	Serves 4 to 6	1 cup (190 g) Black Japonica rice 2⅓ cups (550 ml) water	Rinse the rice first. Coat the rice cooker bowl with nonstick cooking spray or a film of vegetable oil (this is important with this rice). When the machine switches to the Keep Warm cycle, open and dry the inside of the cover. Close the cover and let the rice rest for 30 to 45 minutes. Fluff the rice a few times with a wooden or plastic rice paddle or wooden spoon.

1

BREAKFASTS

Creamy Breakfast Oatmeal 12

Old-Fashioned Steel-Cut Oatmeal 15

Vanilla Oatmeal Crème Brûlée with Berries 16

Hot Apple Granola 18

Maple-Cinnamon Rice Pudding 21

Sweet Breakfast Grits with Fresh Fruit 22

Rice and Sweet Potato Porridge 25

Thanksgiving Jook 26

CREAMY BREAKFAST OATMEAL

MACHINE: Medium (6-cup [990 g]) rice cooker; fuzzy logic only

CYCLE: Porridge

SERVES: 2

Oats have a reputation for contributing to health similar to a homeopathic cure. Oats and milk are said to ward off the worst of chills, as well as making a great poultice-like mask for the face. With maple syrup and sweet dried dates, plain old oatmeal is a morning feast that raises its status above that of a humble grain. Note that this recipe calls for steel-cut oats rather than rolled oats, making an exceptionally creamy porridge.

....

1. Place the oats, vanilla milk, cinnamon, salt, and maple syrup in the rice cooker bowl; stir gently to combine. Sprinkle with the dates. Close the cover and set for the Porridge cycle.

2. At the end of the cycle, the cereal will be thick and will hold on Keep Warm for up to 1 hour. Spoon into bowls and serve hot.

⅔ cup (117 g) steel-cut oats

1¾ cups (410 ml) milk mixed with 1 teaspoon pure vanilla extract or 1¾ cups (410 ml) vanilla soy milk

1¼ teaspoons ground cinnamon

Pinch of fine sea salt

2 tablespoons (30 ml) pure maple syrup

¼ cup (45 g) chopped dates

1¼ cups (220 g) steel-cut oats

3 cups (705 ml) cold water

Pinch of sea salt

Pure maple syrup and cold milk, for serving

OLD-FASHIONED STEEL-CUT OATMEAL

MACHINE: Medium (6-cup [990 g]) rice cooker; fuzzy logic only

CYCLE: Porridge

SERVES: 3

Steel-cut oats are much chewier than regular rolled oats and the cooking time is considerably longer, but the rice cooker is perfect for cooking the hearty, old-fashioned grain, especially after an overnight soak. If you like your oatmeal creamy, substitute 1 cup (235 ml) of milk for 1 cup (235 ml) of the water.

1. The night before serving, place the oats, water, and salt in a lidded bowl or the rice cooker bowl. Cover and set aside at room temperature until morning.

2. In the morning, pour the mixture with its liquid into the rice cooker bowl, if necessary; stir gently to combine. Close the cover and set for the Porridge cycle. At the end of the cycle, the cereal will be thick and will hold on Keep Warm for 1 to 2 hours.

3. Spoon into bowls and serve hot, with a drizzle of maple syrup and the milk.

VANILLA OATMEAL CRÈME BRÛLÉE WITH BERRIES

MACHINE: Medium (6-cup [990 g]) or large (10-cup [1.7 kg]) rice cooker; fuzzy logic only

CYCLE: Porridge

SERVES: 4

Crème brûlée oatmeal is the new darling of the bed and breakfast/restaurant brunch set, taking this breakfast staple from rustic to sophisticated. Usually the oatmeal is baked, but here the cooking is done in the rice cooker. The richly flavored oatmeal is topped with the caramelized sugar crust that is characteristic of the dessert custard of the same name. You can make this in the winter with soaked raisins or dried cranberries and toasted walnuts or almonds in place of the berries. Serve it for company but be prepared, as it is addictive.

1½ cups (120 g) old-fashioned rolled oats (not quick-cooking)

3 cups (705 ml) milk or half-and-half (you can substitute water for part of this) or soy milk

2 teaspoons vanilla extract

¼ teaspoon ground cinnamon

Pinch of salt

About 1 cup (weight will vary) fresh berries of your choice, such as blueberries, blackberries, strawberries, and/or raspberries

2 tablespoons (26 g) granulated sugar

1 tablespoon (15 g) packed light brown sugar

⅔ cup (153 g) plain Greek yogurt, (32 g) soy whipped cream, or (48 g) Cool Whip, for topping

1. Place the oats, milk, vanilla, cinnamon, and salt in the rice cooker bowl. Close the cover and set for the Porridge cycle.

2. When the machine switches to the Keep Warm cycle, let the oatmeal steam for 5 minutes. The oatmeal will be semi-thick. With an oversized spoon, fill four 6-ounce (170 g) ramekins, mini soufflé dishes, or custard cups half-full with the oatmeal, then top with a few fresh berries. Spoon the oatmeal over the berries to fill the ramekins to the rim and level each smooth and flat with the back of the spoon. Cool 15 minutes, then cover with plastic wrap and refrigerate until serving time.

3. When ready to serve, preheat the broiler (or you can use a butane kitchen torch). Remove the plastic wrap and place the ramekins on a baking sheet. Combine the 2 sugars in a small bowl, then sprinkle about 2 teaspoons evenly over the top of each ramekin.

4. Set the pan under the broiler 3 inches (7.5 cm) from the heat until the sugar is melted and starting to bubble and turn amber brown, about 1 minute. Watch carefully to avoid burning. Remove from the oven and let stand for 5 minutes to cool the sugar. Crack the crispy tops and serve topped with more fresh berries and a dollop of yogurt, soy whipped cream, or Cool Whip. Eat out of the ramekin while warm.

2 cups (372 g) cooked white rice

2½ cups (590 ml) milk

¼ cup (60 ml) heavy cream or milk

¼ cup (60 ml) pure maple syrup

¼ cup (40 g) dried tart cherries, (30 g) dried cranberries, or (35 g) raisins

¼ teaspoon ground cinnamon

Pinch of freshly grated nutmeg

Pinch of fine sea salt

MAPLE-CINNAMON RICE PUDDING

MACHINE: Medium (6-cup [990 g]) rice cooker; fuzzy logic only

CYCLE: Porridge

SERVES: 3 to 4

This is a creamy breakfast rice pudding that is perfectly addictive. It can also be made with long-grain brown rice, but the white rice is the creamiest and most nurturing. Serve with pure maple syrup or sliced or chopped fresh or canned fruit, such as bananas, berries, or peaches.

1. The night before serving, combine the rice, milk, cream, maple syrup, dried fruit, spices, and salt in a bowl. Cover and refrigerate until morning.

2. In the morning, coat the rice cooker bowl with butter-flavored nonstick cooking spray. Pour the soaked rice mixture into the rice bowl; stir gently to combine. Close the cover and set for the Porridge cycle.

3. At the end of the cycle, the cereal will be thick and creamy; let it steam on Keep Warm for 10 minutes. Spoon into bowls and serve immediately.

SWEET BREAKFAST GRITS WITH FRESH FRUIT

MACHINE: Medium (6-cup [990 g]) rice cooker; fuzzy logic only

CYCLE: Porridge

SERVES: 3

When you see the word *grits*, it is easy to assume it means cracked hominy grits made from cornmeal, but in reality *grits* can refer to any coarsely cracked grain, including millet, corn, oats, or barley. Grits can be in a fine, medium, or coarse grind; the finer the grind, the faster it cooks. Here old-fashioned grits ground from corn are cooked in milk and are perfect for the breakfast table. The stone-ground grits will have much more flavor than the quick-cooking variety.

....

1. Place the grits, milk, honey, and salt in the rice cooker bowl; stir gently to combine. Close the cover and set for the Porridge cycle.

2. At the end of the cycle, the cereal will be thick and creamy, and will hold on Keep Warm for 1 to 2 hours. Spoon into bowls and serve hot, topped with the fruit.

¾ cup (120 g) stone-ground or quick-cooking yellow or white grits

2½ cups (590 ml) milk

3 to 4 tablespoons (60 to 80 g) honey

½ teaspoon fine sea salt

Hulled and sliced fresh strawberries, blackberries, blueberries, or peeled, pitted, and sliced peaches, sprinkled with a teaspoon or two of sugar, for topping

¾ cup (150 g) or 1 rice cooker cup Japanese-style short- or medium-grain white rice

1 cup (110 g) peeled and chopped sweet potato (chop the pieces about ¾ inch (1.9 cm) on a side; you will need about 1 small sweet potato)

5 cups (1.2 L) water

Salt (optional)

RICE AND SWEET POTATO PORRIDGE

MACHINE: Medium (6-cup [990 g]) rice cooker; fuzzy logic only

CYCLE: Porridge

SERVES: 2 to 4

Sweet potatoes are a wintertime fixture in Japan, where they are sold by vendors on the street. This recipe for an almost-plain porridge is livened up with tender sweet potatoes. If you are ailing, you'd want to eat this plain. If you're not, you might like it with a sprinkle of toasted Japanese sesame seeds or green onion, or a drizzle of sesame oil.

1. Wash the rice. Place the rice in a bowl (or use the bowl of your rice cooker) and fill the bowl about half-full with cold tap water. Swirl the rice in the water with your hand. Carefully pour off most of the water, holding one cupped hand under the stream to catch any grains of rice that are carried away with the water. Holding the bowl steady with one hand, use the other to rub and squeeze the wet rice, turning the bowl as you go, so that all the rice is "scrubbed." The small amount of water in the bowl will turn chalky white. Now, run cold water into the bowl, give the rice a quick swish, and carefully drain off the water as before. Repeat the scrubbing and pouring-off process two more times. By the third time, the water you pour off will be nearly clear.

2. Place the drained rice, sweet potato, and water in the rice cooker bowl. Close the cover and set for the Porridge cycle.

3. When the machine switches to the Keep Warm cycle, stir the porridge with a wooden or plastic rice paddle or wooden spoon. Serve immediately, ladling the porridge into small bowls. Add salt to taste, if desired.

THANKSGIVING JOOK

MACHINE: Medium (6-cup [990 g]) rice cooker; fuzzy logic only

CYCLE: Porridge

SERVES: 4 to 6

You don't really have to wait for Thanksgiving to make this recipe. Make it any time a big party leaves you with a turkey or duck carcass, a big hambone, or some other leftover that is just too good to throw away.

....

1. Make the stock. Put the carcass into a soup pot, breaking or cutting it into 2 to 4 pieces if necessary to fit. Add the water, using more if necessary so that all or most of the carcass is submerged. Add the onion and ginger. Bring the water to a boil over high heat, cover the pot, and let the stock simmer for 2 hours, until the meat is falling away from the bones. If you are not making jook right away, let the stock cool, uncovered, then cover the pot and refrigerate it for several hours or overnight.

2. When you are ready to make the jook, skim off any fat from the surface of the stock. Strain the stock. Dice or shred 1 cup (140 g) of the turkey meat and reserve it. Discard the rest of the meat. Discard the turkey bones and skin, onion, and ginger.

3. Wash the rice. Place the rice in a bowl (or use the bowl of your rice cooker) and fill the bowl about half-full with cold tap water. Swirl the rice in the water with your hand. Carefully pour off most of the water, holding one cupped hand under the stream to catch any grains of rice that are carried away with the water. Holding the bowl steady with one hand, use the other to rub and squeeze the wet rice, turning the bowl as you go, so that all the rice is "scrubbed." The small amount of water in the bowl will turn chalky white. Now, run cold water into the bowl, give the rice a quick swish, and carefully drain off the water as before. Repeat the scrubbing and pouring-off process two more times. By the third time, the water you pour off will be nearly clear.

STOCK

1 medium-size turkey carcass

About 12 cups (2.8 L) water

1 small onion, quartered

1 piece (1 inch, or 2.5 cm) of fresh ginger, cut into 4 pieces and each piece lightly crushed

RICE

¾ cup (150 g) or 1 rice cooker cup Japanese-style short- or medium-grain white rice

2 cups (150 g) shredded Napa cabbage

1 cup (130 g) diced carrot (about 2 medium-size carrots)

Some or all of the following, for topping: sliced green onions, chopped fresh cilantro leaves, peeled and grated fresh ginger, sesame oil, a few drops of soy sauce, salt

4. Place the drained rice in the rice cooker bowl. Add 4½ cups (1.1 L) of the stock, or use a combination of stock and water if there is not enough stock. Add the cabbage and carrot. Close the cover and set for the Porridge cycle.

5. When the machine switches to the Keep Warm cycle, stir in the diced turkey; let the jook steam for 10 minutes. Serve immediately, with any or all of the toppings.

2

EVERYDAY RICE

Greek Lemon and Dill Rice with Feta 30

Rice with Fresh Greens for a Crowd 33

Japanese White Rice with Umeboshi and Sesame 34

Basmati Rice with Corn and Peas 37

Chinese Sausage and Rice 38

Indonesian Rice Bowl 40

Wild Rice and Bulgur with Leeks and Toasted Almonds 43

GREEK LEMON AND DILL RICE WITH FETA

MACHINE: Medium (6-cup [990 g]) rice cooker; fuzzy logic or on/off

CYCLE: Regular

SERVES: 3 to 4

The Greeks have a culinary love affair with the mating of lemon and dill, two plants that have been used since antiquity (lemon trees were planted along the Tigris and Euphrates rivers). Dill is native to the eastern Mediterranean and contains a flavor element called limonene, which is a natural flavor complement to lemon. In Greek cooking, you find this combination in everything from soups to meat dishes. Rice is no exception. The mint is an optional ingredient, but a traditional one. This dish is also good made with brown rice; if you use it, increase the amount of chicken stock to 2⅔ cups (630 ml).

1½ cups (278 g) long-grain white rice, such as basmati, Jasmati, Carolina, or jasmine

2 cups (470 ml) chicken stock

2 tablespoons (30 ml) olive oil

2 small white boiling onions, chopped

¼ cup (35 g) pine nuts

¼ cup (60 ml) fresh lemon juice

1 tablespoon (4 g) minced fresh dill or 1 teaspoon dillweed

1½ teaspoons minced fresh mint leaves or ½ teaspoon dried mint leaves, crumbled

1 cup (150 g) crumbled feta cheese

1 lemon, cut into 8 wedges

1. Coat the rice cooker bowl with nonstick cooking spray or a film of olive oil. Place the rice in the rice bowl. Add the stock; swirl to combine. Close the cover and set for the Regular cycle.

2. When the machine switches to the Keep Warm cycle, let the rice steam for 10 minutes.

3. While the rice is steaming, in a small skillet, heat the olive oil over medium heat. Add the onions and cook, stirring, until translucent and softened, about 5 minutes. Add the pine nuts and cook, stirring constantly, until golden brown (it won't take long).

4. When the steaming period is finished, add the sautéed mixture to the rice bowl, along with the lemon juice, dill, and mint. Stir with a wooden or plastic rice paddle or wooden spoon to evenly distribute. Close the cover and let the rice steam for an additional 10 minutes on the Keep Warm cycle.

5. Serve the rice immediately, topped with some feta cheese and a lemon wedge on the side.

NOTE

This rice will hold on Keep Warm for 1 to 2 hours, if necessary, but don't add the lemon juice, dill, and mint until 10 minutes before you plan to serve.

6 cups (1.1 kg) long-grain white rice, such as basmati, Texmati, converted, or Carolina

7¾ cups (1.8 L) water

5 tablespoons (70 g) unsalted butter, cut into pieces

1¼ tablespoons (20 g) salt

½ cup (20 g) chopped fresh Italian parsley leaves

½ cup (48 g) chopped fresh mint leaves

½ cup (20 g) chopped fresh basil leaves

RICE WITH FRESH GREENS FOR A CROWD

MACHINE: Large (10-cup [1.7 kg]) rice cooker; fuzzy logic or on/off

CYCLE: Regular

SERVES: 20 to 24

This recipe is perfect for entertaining; the combination of parsley, mint, and basil is very Italian and ever so good with grilled fish and chicken. Remember that, whenever cooking rice to the full capacity of the cooker bowl, the rice on the bottom will be a bit squishy, so a thorough but gentle mixing after the steaming period is imperative.

1. Place the rice in a fine strainer or bowl, rinse with cold water until the water runs clear, and drain.

2. Coat the rice cooker bowl with nonstick cooking spray or a film of vegetable oil. Place the rice in the rice bowl. Add the water, butter, and salt; swirl just to combine. Close the cover and set for the Regular cycle.

3. When the machine switches to the Keep Warm cycle, let the rice steam for 15 minutes. Add the herbs to the rice bowl; stir with a wooden or plastic rice paddle or wooden spoon to evenly distribute. Close the cover and let the rice steam for 30 minutes. This rice will hold on Keep Warm for up to 2 hours. Serve hot.

JAPANESE WHITE RICE WITH UMEBOSHI AND SESAME

SERVES: 2 to 3

Tart and salty, pinky-red umeboshi pickled plums are an acquired taste to some. To others, it is just another comfort food along with miso. Anyone who has taken a macrobiotic cooking class gets hooked on umeboshi. Prepare the condiments while the rice is cooking; you want to be ready to serve as soon as the rice has finished on the Keep Warm cycle. Umeboshi plums are sold in Asian groceries and natural foods stores. This recipe—inspired by Hiroko Shimbo, author of *The Japanese Kitchen* (Harvard Common Press, 2000)—has quickly become a favorite quick lunch on the run.

1. Place the umeboshi, parsley, and sesame seeds in separate small, shallow serving bowls.

2. Place the rice in a medium-size serving bowl, sprinkle it with the condiments, and drizzle with some sesame oil and tamari. Serve immediately.

2 umeboshi plums, pitted and minced

2 tablespoons (8 g) minced fresh Italian parsley leaves

1½ tablespoons (8 g) toasted Japanese sesame seeds

3 cups (558 g) hot cooked medium-grain white rice

Sesame oil (not toasted), for drizzling

Tamari (a thick, strong soy sauce; reduced-sodium, if desired), for drizzling

NOTE

Japanese sesame seeds are sold toasted; you can toast them again in a dry skillet for more flavor.

1 cup (190 g) white
basmati rice

1½ cups (355 ml) water

½ teaspoon salt

2 tablespoons (8 g) chopped
fresh Italian parsley leaves

1 teaspoon paprika

½ cup (80 g) finely chopped
red onion

½ cup (75 g) fresh or (65 g)
frozen English peas, shelled

½ cup (75 g) fresh or (65 g)
frozen (and thawed) corn
kernels

BASMATI RICE
WITH CORN AND PEAS

MACHINE: Medium (6-cup [990 g]) rice cooker; fuzzy logic or on/off

CYCLE: Regular

SERVES: 3 to 4

This is an easy dinner to have on standby when you can't think of anything
else to make. Add your protein of choice to make this a heartier meal, or
add other frozen vegetables that are taking up space in your freezer.

1. Place the rice in a fine strainer or bowl, rinse with cold water until the
water runs clear, and drain.

2. Coat the rice cooker bowl with nonstick cooking spray or a film
of vegetable oil. Place the rice in the rice bowl. Add the remaining
ingredients; stir just to combine. Cover and set for the Regular cycle.

3. When the machine switches to the Keep Warm cycle, let the rice
steam for 10 minutes. Fluff the rice with a wooden or plastic rice paddle
or wooden spoon. This rice will hold on Keep Warm for up to 1 hour.
Serve hot.

CHINESE SAUSAGE AND RICE

MACHINE: Medium (6-cup [990 g]) rice cooker; fuzzy logic or on/off

CYCLE: Regular

SERVES: 4

Food historian and cookbook author Barbara Grunes uses her rice cooker for her home meals. Her recipe for chewy medium-grain rice with spicy Chinese sausage and cilantro is good by itself or as a side dish to serve with other Asian-style foods. The sweet Chinese pork sausage is seasoned with sugar, salt, and wine (look for it in the refrigerator case in Asian markets). If you want to vary the flavor, use cooked Italian sausage and basil instead of the green onions, cilantro, and sesame seeds. The sausage gently flavors the rice as it cooks. Look for black sesame seeds in Asian markets. If you can't find them, use Japanese or regular white sesame seeds. The Japanese ones are more flavorful. This is a super-easy, satisfying dish.

2 cups (390 g) medium-grain white rice

1 cup (240 g) Chinese sausage (*lop cheon*), thinly sliced on the diagonal

½ cup (50 g) thinly sliced green onions, mostly green parts

2¾ cups (645 ml) water

¼ cup (4 g) chopped fresh cilantro leaves, for garnish

2 tablespoons (16 g) black sesame seeds (*goma*), for garnish

1. Place the rice in a fine strainer or bowl, rinse with cold water until the water runs clear, and drain.

2. Coat the rice cooker bowl with nonstick cooking spray or a film of vegetable oil. Place the rice, sausage, and green onions in the rice bowl. Add the water; stir just to combine. Close the cover and set for the Regular cycle.

3. When the machine switches to the Keep Warm cycle, let the rice steam for 15 minutes. Fluff the rice with a wooden or plastic rice paddle or wooden spoon.

4. Serve immediately. Spoon the rice mixture into a deep serving bowl and sprinkle with the cilantro and then the sesame seeds.

INDONESIAN RICE BOWL

MACHINE: Medium (6-cup [990 g]) rice cooker; fuzzy logic or on/off

CYCLE: Regular

SERVES: 4

From one of the Bay Area's favorite food writers, backyard gardeners, and seed purveyors, Renee Shepherd, comes this satisfying one-dish meal adapted from her book *Recipes from a Kitchen Garden* (Ten Speed, 1993). This is a great recipe to use up leftover chicken. The popular peanut sauce is one of the definitive tastes of Thai cuisines. This simplified version of the *rijsttafel* table, a popular full-rice meal in Indonesia, looks incredibly festive served with all the condiments.

1. Make the rice: Coat the rice cooker bowl with nonstick cooking spray or a film of vegetable oil. Place the rice in the rice bowl. Add the water; swirl to combine. Close the cover and set for the Regular cycle.

2. Make the sauce: In a medium-size saucepan, combine all the sauce ingredients. Cook over low heat, stirring a few times, until the mixture achieves a saucelike consistency. Cover and keep warm.

3. When the machine switches to the Keep Warm cycle, sprinkle the peas and chicken on top of the rice. Close the cover and let the rice steam for 20 minutes.

4. Transfer the rice mixture to a warmed serving platter with sloped sides. Pour the hot stock and peanut sauce over the rice. Stir gently to combine the peas and chicken with the stock and peanut sauce. Sprinkle with the green onion tops and peanuts. Serve immediately with a choice of condiments.

1 cup (180 g) Thai jasmine rice

1 cup (235 ml) plus 2 tablespoons (30 ml) water

2½ cups (375 g) fresh or (325 g) frozen petite peas (2 pounds [900 g] fresh unshelled)

2½ cups (313 g) shredded poached chicken breast

½ cup (120 ml) hot chicken stock

SAUCE

⅓ cup (87 g) creamy peanut butter

½ cup (120 ml) chicken broth or water

1 tablespoon (15 ml) dry sherry

2 tablespoons (30 ml) rice vinegar

2 teaspoons peeled and grated fresh ginger

⅛ teaspoon cayenne pepper

½ teaspoon sugar

1 clove garlic, minced

2 green onions, white parts only, minced (chop the green tops for garnish)

½ cup (75 g) chopped roasted peanuts, for garnish

CONDIMENTS

Separate small bowls of chutney, sliced bananas, raisins, unsweetened shredded coconut, minced fresh cilantro leaves, mandarin orange segments, chopped apples, plain yogurt

½ stick (¼ cup [55 g]) unsalted butter

5 small leeks, white parts only, washed well and thinly sliced

1½ cups (240 g) wild rice

3⅓ cups (785 ml) chicken stock

¼ teaspoon salt

½ cup (70 g) bulgur cracked wheat

1 cup (235 ml) boiling water

½ cup (55 g) slivered blanched almonds

WILD RICE AND BULGUR WITH LEEKS AND TOASTED ALMONDS

MACHINE: Medium (6-cup [990 g]) rice cooker; fuzzy logic or on/off

CYCLE: Quick Cook and/or Brown Rice or Regular

SERVES: 8

Here wild rice and bulgur are cooked together with leeks and almonds, a winning—and very French—culinary mating.

....

1. Set the rice cooker for the Quick Cook or Brown Rice or Regular cycle. Place the butter in the rice cooker bowl. When melted, add the leeks and cook, stirring a few times, until softened, about 3 minutes. Add the rice, stock, and salt; stir just to combine. Close the cover and reset for the Brown Rice or Regular cycle or let the Brown Rice or Regular cycle complete.

2. Meanwhile, in a small bowl, cover the bulgur with the boiling water. Let stand on the counter to soften while the rice is cooking.

3. Preheat the oven to 325°F (170°C, or gas mark 3).

4. Place the almonds on a baking sheet and toast until just golden, 5 to 7 minutes. Remove from the sheet and set aside.

5. When the machine switches to the Keep Warm cycle, drain the bulgur, pressing to remove any excess liquid. Open the cover and stir in the almonds and bulgur, using a wooden or plastic rice paddle or wooden spoon. Close the cover and let the grains steam for 15 minutes. This dish will hold on Keep Warm for up to 1 hour. Serve hot.

3

BEANS, LEGUMES, AND VEGETABLES

Italian White Beans 46
Frijoles Negros 49
Hummus 50
Broccoli with Lemon Sauce 53
Herbed Green Beans 54
Steamed Corn on the Cob.. 57
Spiced Yams with Ginger and Pears.................................... 58

ITALIAN WHITE BEANS

MACHINE: Medium (6-cup [990 g]) or large (10-cup [1.7 kg]) rice cooker; fuzzy logic or on/off

CYCLE: Quick Cook and/or Regular

MAKES: About 3 cups (510 g)

SERVES: 6

The large oval white kidney bean, also called cannellini, is a favorite home-cooked bean. It has a delicate, sweet flavor and cooks up nice and firm. These beans are a great side dish for fish and meats.

....

1. Place the olive oil, onion, and meat in the rice cooker bowl. Set the rice cooker for the Quick Cook or Regular cycle and cook for about 15 minutes, stirring a few times. Add the carrot and celery and cook for another 10 minutes to soften slightly, stirring a few times.

2. Add the beans, then add the chicken stock and herbs; stir to combine. Close the cover, reset for the Regular cycle, and set a timer for 1¼ to 1½ hours.

3. When the timer sounds, remove the meat and bay leaves and taste for doneness. Season the beans with salt and pepper to taste and serve immediately.

¼ cup (60 ml) olive oil

1 medium-size yellow onion, cut into 8 wedges

1 large piece of prosciutto rind or 1 small smoked ham hock

1 large carrot, cut into thick slices

2 stalks celery, with leaves, cut into chunks

1 cup (202 g) dried cannellini beans, picked over, rinsed, soaked in water to cover (overnight or quick-soak method), and drained

3 cups (705 ml) chicken stock

2 bay leaves

Pinch of dried thyme

Salt

Freshly ground black pepper

1 pound (about 2 cups [455 g]) dried black beans, picked over, rinsed, soaked in water to cover (overnight or quick-soak method), and drained

1 medium-size yellow onion, finely chopped

1 medium-size green or red bell pepper, seeded and finely chopped

1 or 2 fresh jalapeño chiles, seeded and minced

½ teaspoon ground cumin

1 bay leaf

½ cup (123 g) tomato sauce or (130 g) salsa

2 quarts (1.9 L) water

1 tablespoon (15 ml) red wine vinegar

Salt

FRIJOLES NEGROS

MACHINE: Medium (6-cup [990 g]) or large (10-cup [1.7 kg]) rice cooker; fuzzy logic or on/off

CYCLE: Regular

MAKES: About 4 cups (688 g)

SERVES: 8

Black beans, also known as turtle beans, are the cornerstone of Central and South American soul food, just like the pinto bean is in Mexican cooking. Once a specialty item, black beans are now seen in every supermarket. They have an appealing, rather addictive, natural flavor and are easy to digest. If you like a smoky edge to your black beans, add two canned chipotle chiles. Float a few tablespoons (45 to 60 ml) of olive oil on top of the cooked beans before serving.

....

1. Place the beans, onion, bell pepper, jalapeño, cumin, bay leaf, tomato sauce or salsa, and water in the rice cooker bowl. Close the cover, set for the Regular cycle, and set a timer for 1½ hours.

2. When the timer sounds, you will have plenty of liquid with the cooked beans. Taste the beans for doneness. Remove the bay leaf. Stir in the vinegar, season with salt to taste, and serve immediately.

HUMMUS

MACHINE: Medium (6-cup [990 g]) or large (10-cup [1.7 kg]) rice cooker; fuzzy logic or on/off

CYCLE: Regular

MAKES: 3 cups (738 g)

SERVES: 12 as an appetizer

To serve, make a depression in the top of the hummus and drizzle with olive oil until it runs down the sides and pools in the side of the dish. Place spears of romaine lettuce all around for dipping. Give each person a whole fresh pita bread to tear and scoop up this dip.

1 cup (200 g) dried chickpeas, picked over, rinsed, soaked in water to cover (overnight or quick-soak method), and drained

Salt

2 to 3 cloves garlic, or more to taste, peeled

¼ to ⅓ cup (60 to 80 ml) fresh lemon juice

⅓ cup (80 g) sesame paste (tahini)

¼ cup (60 ml) extra-virgin olive oil

Pinch of cayenne pepper

1. Place the chickpeas in the rice cooker bowl and cover with 3 inches (7.5 cm) of water. Close the cover, set for the Regular cycle, and set a timer for 1½ hours. During the last half hour of cooking, season with salt to taste.

2. When the timer sounds, test the beans for doneness. Drain the beans, reserving the liquid.

3. In a food processor, finely chop the garlic. Add the warm chickpeas and pulse to mash them. Add the lemon juice, sesame paste, olive oil, and cayenne and, while the machine is running, slowly add ⅓ cup (80 ml) of the reserved cooking liquid through the feed tube until you get a fluffy, smooth consistency. Taste and adjust the flavors.

4. Transfer to a serving bowl and serve immediately, or refrigerate, covered, until ready to serve.

2 pounds (900 g) broccoli, cut into equal-size florets and stems peeled and cut into pieces the size of the florets

LEMON SAUCE

1 small clove garlic, peeled

1 large egg

2 teaspoons Dijon mustard

2 tablespoons (30 ml) fresh lemon juice

¼ teaspoon salt

Pinch of cayenne pepper

¼ cup (60 ml) olive oil

½ cup (120 ml) canola or vegetable oil

BROCCOLI WITH LEMON SAUCE

MACHINE: Large (10-cup [1.7 kg]) rice cooker; on/off only

CYCLE: Regular

SERVES: 6

This lemon sauce is really a mayonnaise and a favorite one at that. It is the perfect sauce for fresh broccoli. Once you make homemade mayo, you will understand why this sauce is one of the most beloved in the kitchen. You can substitute orange juice for the lemon. Because the lemon sauce contains raw egg, make sure you use the freshest egg possible, that you keep it refrigerated until ready to serve, and that you eat this the day you make it. Also, because of the possibility of salmonella, it's best not to serve this to small children, the elderly, or anyone with a compromised immune system.

1. Fill the rice cooker bowl about one-quarter full of hot water. Close the cover and set for the Regular cycle.

2. Coat the steamer basket with nonstick cooking spray and place the broccoli in the basket. When the water comes to a boil, place the steamer basket in the cooker and close the cover. Steam until crisp-tender, 12 to 18 minutes.

3. While the broccoli steams, make the Lemon Sauce. In a food processor with the motor running, drop the garlic in through the feed tube to chop. Stop the machine and add the egg, mustard, lemon juice, salt, and cayenne; pulse a few times to combine. With the machine running, slowly drizzle in the oils through the feed tube; the mixture will thicken and be smooth. If you are not using the sauce right away, transfer it to a covered container and refrigerate until ready to serve.

4. Serve small spoonfuls of the Lemon Sauce on the warm broccoli.

HERBED GREEN BEANS

MACHINE: Large (10-cup [1.7 kg]) rice cooker; on/off only

CYCLE: Regular

SERVES: 4

These are the very best green beans. Diners say "ho-hum" when they think about having green beans for dinner, but one taste of these savory herbed vegetables and, trust us, they will be all eaten up.

....

1. Fill the rice cooker bowl about one-quarter full of hot water. Close the cover and set for the Regular cycle.

2. Coat the steamer basket with nonstick cooking spray and place the beans in the basket. When the water comes to a boil, place the steamer basket in the cooker and close the cover. Steam until crisp-tender, 7 to 10 minutes.

3. Meanwhile, in a medium-size skillet, heat the butter and olive oil together over medium heat until the butter melts. Add the onion and celery and cook, stirring a few times, until just softened, about 2 minutes. Add the parsley, rosemary, basil, and pepper strips, cover, and cook for 5 minutes; don't let the pepper strips get too soft. Add salt to taste.

4. Add the steamed beans to the skillet and toss to combine. Transfer to a shallow 1-quart casserole that is ovenproof or microwave-safe. Serve immediately, or make a few hours ahead, cover, and reheat in the oven or microwave to serve.

1 pound (455 g) fresh green beans, ends trimmed

2 tablespoons (28 g) unsalted butter

2 tablespoons (30 ml) olive oil

½ cup (80 g) minced onion

¼ cup (30 g) minced celery

¼ cup (10 g) minced fresh Italian parsley leaves

1 teaspoon chopped fresh rosemary leaves or ¼ teaspoon dried rosemary leaves, crumbled

¼ teaspoon dried basil leaves, crumbled

½ to 1 medium-size red bell pepper (depending on whether you want just a touch of color or some to eat with each bite), seeded and cut into strips

Salt

Corn on the cob bought at a farmers' market or roadside stand, 1 to 2 ears for each diner, husked

Unsalted butter

Salt or salt-free herb blend, such as Mrs. Dash

STEAMED CORN ON THE COB

MACHINE: Large (10-cup [1.7 kg]) rice cooker; on/off only

CYCLE: Regular

There is fresh, white, and very young (oh, Silver Queen) corn or corn picked a bit later, yellow and less juicy. Early season, mid-season, or late season, corn on the cob is summer incarnate. Shuck the ears by holding the stem end over the garbage can and discard the messy silks and husk before this simple steaming.

1. Fill the rice cooker bowl about one-quarter full of hot water. Close the cover and set for the Regular cycle.

2. Coat the steamer baskets with nonstick cooking spray or line with a layer of corn husks. Arrange the whole ears of corn in the steamer baskets, side by side, with a bit of room in between and broken in half to fill the ends, if desired. When the water comes to a boil, place the steamer baskets in the cooker and close the cover. Steam until tender, 10 to 15 minutes, depending on the size and age of the corn.

3. Remove the corn from the steamer and serve immediately with butter and a shaker of salt.

SPICED YAMS WITH GINGER AND PEARS

MACHINE: Large (10-cup [1.7 kg]) rice cooker; on/off only

CYCLE: Regular

SERVES: 6

Although yams are great just plain with butter, here is one step beyond in case you need a special holiday dish. The pears give it a lot of sweetness, so balance with another vegetable, such as green beans or zucchini, in your menu.

....

1. Preheat the oven to 350°F (180°C, or gas mark 4). Fill the rice cooker bowl about one-quarter full of hot water. Close the cover and set for the Regular cycle.

2. Coat the steamer basket with nonstick cooking spray and place the yams in the basket. When the water comes to a boil, place the steamer basket in the cooker and close the cover. Steam until soft enough to mash, 10 to 15 minutes.

3. Transfer the yams to a large bowl. With a fork, coarsely mash the yams with the ginger, cardamom, and salt. Fold in the pears. Spoon into a shallow 1½-quart (990 g) gratin dish and smooth the top. (At this point, you can cover the dish and refrigerate for up to 4 hours.) Bake until heated through, 15 to 20 minutes. Serve immediately.

2 pounds (900 g) ruby yams or sweet potatoes, peeled and cut into 2-inch (5 cm) chunks

2 teaspoons peeled and grated fresh ginger

1 teaspoon ground cardamom

Pinch of salt

3 firm ripe pears, peeled, cored, diced, and drizzled with the juice of 1 small lemon to prevent discoloration

4

POLENTA, GRITS, AND HOMINY

Traditional Grits 62
Creamy Old-Fashioned Grits 65
Shrimp and Grits 66
Fried Grits 69
Fresh Hominy... 70
Italian Polenta 73
French Polenta 74
Small-Portion Polenta 77

TRADITIONAL GRITS

MACHINE: Medium (6-cup [990 g]) rice cooker; fuzzy logic (preferred) or on/off

CYCLE: Porridge or Regular

SERVES: 4

If you live outside the southern part of the US, the only grits you will find in the supermarket will be instant or quick-cooking. Luckily, there are excellent mail-order sources for fresh ground grits. Fresh ground grits are speckled from the bits of grain left over from the milling, so be sure to cover them first with water and let the husks rise to the top, then drain and proceed from the beginning of the recipe. If you want to use quick-cooking grits, just cook for one cycle in the rice cooker and they will still be very good.

....

1. If you'd like to remove the husks, combine the grits and some cold tap water in a bowl or use the rice cooker bowl; the husks will rise to the top and can be skimmed off. Drain the grits.

2. Place the grits, water, and salt in the rice cooker bowl; stir for 15 seconds with a wooden or plastic rice paddle or wooden spoon. Close the cover and set for the Porridge or Regular cycle. A few times during the cooking, open the cover and stir for 15 seconds, then close the cover.

3. At the end of the Porridge cycle, reset for a second Porridge cycle, giving the grits two full cycles to reach the optimum consistency.

4. At the end of the second Porridge cycle, or when the Regular cycle completes, stir in the butter, season to taste with pepper, and serve hot. These grits will hold on Keep Warm for up to 2 hours.

1 cup (140 g) coarse stone-ground grits

3 cups (705 ml) water

½ teaspoon salt

3 tablespoons (42 g) unsalted butter

Ground white pepper

NOTE

Creamy Traditional Grits: Replace 1 cup (235 ml) of the water with 1 cup (235 ml) of whole milk and omit the white pepper. This version is good served with pure maple syrup and chopped crisp bacon.

1 cup (140 g) coarse stone-ground grits

3 cups (705 ml) water

½ teaspoon salt

2 tablespoons (28 g) unsalted butter, divided

¼ cup (60 ml) heavy cream

CREAMY OLD-FASHIONED GRITS

MACHINE: Medium (6-cup [990 g]) rice cooker; fuzzy logic (preferred) or on/off

CYCLE: Porridge or Regular

SERVES: 4

Adding a small amount of cream at the end of cooking makes these grits that little bit more special for a breakfast side dish with eggs or as a hot cereal.

....

1. Combine the grits and some cold tap water in a bowl or use the rice cooker bowl; the husks will rise to the top. Drain through a mesh strainer.

2. Place the grits, water, salt, and 1 tablespoon (14 g) of the butter in the rice cooker bowl; stir for 15 seconds with a wooden or plastic rice paddle or wooden spoon. Close the cover and set for the Porridge or Regular cycle. A few times during the cooking, open the cover and stir for 15 seconds, then close the cover.

3. At the end of the Porridge cycle, reset for a second Porridge cycle, giving the grits two full cycles to reach the optimum consistency.

4. At the end of the second Porridge cycle, or when the Regular cycle completes, open the cover and stir in the remaining 1 tablespoon (14 g) butter and the cream. Stir quickly, close the cover, and allow the grits to rest at least until the butter melts, about 10 minutes. These grits will hold on Keep Warm for up to 1 hour. Stir before serving.

SHRIMP AND GRITS

MACHINE: Medium (6-cup [990 g]) or large (10-cup [1.7 kg]) rice cooker; fuzzy logic (preferred) or on/off

CYCLE: Porridge or Regular

SERVES: 6

Shrimp and grits is real southern coastal Atlantic country food but can now be found served at lots of southern parties and in restaurants. Here is an authentic recipe, just the way they like it in the Carolinas. Run the grits through a third Porridge cycle, if you wish, for a softer consistency.

....

1. Combine the grits and some cold tap water in a bowl or use the rice cooker bowl; the husks will rise to the top. Drain through a mesh strainer.

2. Place the grits, water, and salt in the rice cooker bowl; stir for 15 seconds with a wooden or plastic rice paddle or wooden spoon. Close the cover and set for the Porridge or Regular cycle. A few times during the cooking, open the cover and stir for 15 seconds, then close the cover.

3. At the end of the Porridge cycle, reset for a second Porridge cycle and cook until the grits reach the desired consistency, thick like breakfast porridge. When the right consistency is achieved or the Regular cycle ends, hold on Keep Warm until the shrimp are ready.

2 cups (280 g) coarse stone-ground grits

6 cups (1.4 L) water

1 teaspoon salt

1 stick (½ cup [112 g]) unsalted butter or margarine

¼ cup (60 ml) olive oil

¼ teaspoon Texas Pete or Tabasco hot sauce

1 bay leaf

1 teaspoon pressed garlic

3 tablespoons (45 ml) fresh lemon juice

1 teaspoon minced fresh Italian parsley leaves

1 teaspoon minced fresh chives

½ teaspoon dried tarragon

½ teaspoon dried chervil

½ teaspoon freshly ground black pepper

2 tablespoons (30 ml) Worcestershire sauce

1 pound (455 g) miniature shrimp (90/110 count), shelled and deveined (You can buy these already shelled; look for P&Ds.)

Chopped fresh Italian parsley leaves, for garnish

Chopped fresh chives, for garnish

4. Fifteen minutes before the grits are done, melt the butter in a large sauté pan over medium-high heat. Add the olive oil, hot sauce, bay leaf, garlic, lemon juice, minced parsley, minced chives, tarragon, chervil, pepper, and Worcestershire, bring to a simmer over medium heat, and add the shrimp. Cook, stirring, until the shrimp turn bright pink on both sides, 2 to 3 minutes. Remove the bay leaf.

5. Spoon the hot grits into a large serving bowl. Immediately spoon the shrimp over the grits and drizzle with the sauce from the pan. Sprinkle with the chopped parsley and chives and serve hot.

1½ cups (210 g) coarse stone-ground grits

4 cups (940 ml) water

½ teaspoon salt

¼ cup (56 g) unsalted butter, margarine, or bacon drippings, for frying

Pure maple syrup, for serving

FRIED GRITS

MACHINE: Medium (6-cup [990 g]) rice cooker; fuzzy logic (preferred) or on/off

CYCLE: Porridge or Regular

SERVES: 6

You can't get a more traditional southern breakfast than one with a slice of hot fried grits. This is a great way to use up any leftover grits, but if you are having a few hungry folks in the morning, fried grits, a rasher of bacon, an egg over easy, juice, and hot coffee are a welcome treat.

....

1. Combine the grits and some cold tap water in a bowl or use the rice cooker bowl; the husks will rise to the top. Drain through a mesh strainer.

2. Place the grits, water, and salt in the rice cooker bowl; stir for 15 seconds with a wooden or plastic rice paddle or wooden spoon. Close the cover and set for the Porridge or Regular cycle. A few times during the cooking, open the cover and stir for 15 seconds, then close the cover.

3. When the machine switches to the Keep Warm cycle or the Regular cycle ends, pour the grits into a greased 9 × 5-inch (23 × 13 cm) loaf pan, filling it up to the top. Cover with plastic wrap and refrigerate overnight.

4. The next morning, turn the loaf of grits out of the pan onto a cutting board. With a sharp chef's knife, cut into ½-inch (1.3 cm)-thick slices. Heat a cast-iron or other heavy large skillet over medium-high heat. Place a knob (about 1½ tablespoons [21 g]) of the butter in the pan to melt. Lay the sliced grits in the pan and cook until brown, about 8 minutes on each side, turning once. Add more butter for each new batch, as needed. Remove from the pan with a metal spatula to a serving plate. Serve with the maple syrup.

FRESH HOMINY

MACHINE: Medium (6-cup [990 g]) or large (10-cup [1.7 kg]) rice cooker; fuzzy logic or on/off

CYCLE: Regular

MAKES: About 4 cups (660 g)

Fresh or partially cooked frozen whole hominy needs to be cooked before using. Fresh is usually available in the meat department of supermarkets, especially around the holidays. Do not add any salt while cooking, or the kernels will never soften properly. You can use fresh hominy instead of canned in soups and stews. If you happen to use dried hominy, you will need to double the amount of water and double the cooking time. You can double this recipe in the large-capacity rice cooker.

....

1. Place the hominy in the rice cooker bowl and cover with 2 inches (5 cm) of cold water. Close the cover and set for the Regular cycle. Cook until it is tender and the kernels burst open, but are still slightly firm to the bite, 1 hour or more.

2. Remove the bowl from the rice cooker, drain off most of the liquid by pouring through a colander, and let cool to room temperature. Store in the refrigerator, covered, for up to 2 days.

1 pound (455 g) fresh or frozen hominy, thawed overnight in the refrigerator

4 cups (940 ml) water

1 cup (140 g) coarse-grain yellow polenta

½ teaspoon salt

Freshly ground black pepper

½ stick (¼ cup [55 g]) unsalted butter, or more to taste

⅔ cup (67 g) freshly grated Parmesan cheese (optional)

ITALIAN POLENTA

MACHINE: Medium (6-cup [990 g]) rice cooker; fuzzy logic (preferred) or on/off

CYCLE: Porridge or Regular

SERVES: 4

Italian polenta, the darling of all teachers of Italian cuisine, is labeled *farina di grano turco* on the package, the Italian name of corn since the time of Columbus. It was often made in a traditional copper polenta pot, replete with a special wooden stirring stick, that was handed down within rural families. This is a really nice, fluffy polenta that is foolproof. It uses two full cycles of the Porridge cycle. It thickens considerably during the second cycle and even spits a few times during the cooking. You can double the recipe in a large 10-cup (1.7 kg) machine. Serve with the Parmesan and a pat of garlic butter for a lovely treat, or sprinkle with grated Fontina cheese.

1. Place the water in the rice cooker bowl. Add the polenta and salt; stir for 15 seconds with a wooden or plastic rice paddle or wooden spoon. Close the cover and set for the Porridge or Regular cycle. A few times during the cooking, open the cover, stir for 15 seconds, then close the cover.

2. At the end of the Porridge cycle, reset for a second Porridge cycle; the polenta needs two full cycles to lose its raw, grainy texture. At the end of the second Porridge cycle, or when the Regular cycle completes, taste the polenta and make sure the desired consistency has been reached. Stir in the butter and cheese, if using (if you are chilling the polenta for frying or grilling, or using it under seafood, like grilled pesto prawns, the cheese is not necessary).

3. This polenta will hold on Keep Warm for up to 1 hour, if necessary. Add a bit more hot water if it gets too stiff. Stir before serving.

FRENCH POLENTA

MACHINE: Medium (6-cup [990 g]) or large (10-cup [1.7 kg]) rice cooker; fuzzy logic (preferred) or on/off

CYCLE: Porridge or Regular

SERVES: 6

The French make cornmeal mush, which was originally brought to their country by the armies of the king of Spain in the Middle Ages. Made in all regions of France, the most famous polenta preparation is Savoy mush, and French polenta can sport toppings and additions like roasted game, stewed prunes, cheese, a variety of meat and vegetable sauces, meat pan juices, and truffles, and sometimes is an addition to soup.

2 cups (280 g) coarse-grain yellow polenta

3 cups (705 ml) water

3 cups (705 ml) chicken stock or milk

Salt

Freshly ground black pepper

Freshly grated nutmeg

Sprig thyme, for garnish

....

1. Place the polenta and water in the rice cooker bowl; stir for 15 seconds with a wooden or plastic rice paddle or wooden spoon. Add the stock and salt and pepper and nutmeg to taste. Close the cover and set for the Porridge or Regular cycle. About every 20 minutes, open and stir for 15 seconds, then close the cooker.

2. At the end of the Porridge cycle, reset for a second Porridge cycle; the polenta needs two full cycles to lose its raw, grainy texture. At the end of the second Porridge cycle, or when the Regular cycle completes, taste the polenta to make sure the desired consistency has been reached. This polenta will hold on Keep Warm for up to 1 hour.

3. When ready to serve, spoon onto serving plates and add a sprig of thyme on top.

3 tablespoons (30 g)
coarse-grain yellow polenta

1 cup (235 ml) water

¼ teaspoon salt

Freshly ground black pepper

2 teaspoons unsalted butter

SMALL-PORTION POLENTA

MACHINE: Medium (6-cup [990 g]) rice cooker; fuzzy logic (preferred) or on/off

CYCLE: Porridge or Regular

SERVES: 1 to 2

Sometimes you want just a little bit of hot polenta mush with butter and Parmesan or Asiago cheese to serve as a side dish. This is the perfect recipe.

1. Place the polenta, water, and salt in the rice cooker bowl; stir to combine. Close the cover and set for the Porridge or Regular cycle.

2. At the end of the Porridge cycle, reset for a second Porridge cycle. At the end of the second Porridge cycle, or when the Regular cycle completes, open the cover and add a couple of grinds of black pepper and the butter. Stir quickly, close the cover, and allow the polenta to rest at least until the butter melts. This polenta can be held on Keep Warm for up to 2 hours. Stir before serving.

NOTE

If you are used to buying precooked instant polenta at the store, you are in for a treat if you seek out traditional polenta for this recipe. The corn flavors are richer and deeper and taste more like fresh corn.

5

PILAFS AND RISOTTOS

Bulgur and Cherry Pilaf 80
Rice Pilaf with Fresh Peas 83
Lemon Basmati Pilaf 84
Baby Artichokes and Arborio Rice 87
Butternut Squash Risotto 88
Risotto Milanese 91
Rice Cooker Paella 92

BULGUR AND CHERRY PILAF

MACHINE: Medium (6-cup [990 g]) rice cooker; fuzzy logic or on/off

CYCLE: Quick Cook and/or Regular

SERVES: 4 to 6

Turkish cooking pairs sweet and savory flavor elements, such as rice pilafs with fresh and dried fruit. Here bulgur wheat, which has the most buttery rich flavor of all the grains, is cooked with fresh and dried cherries. Fennel seed is an integral part of Mediterranean cuisine; its flavor just sings in this preparation.

....

1. Set the rice cooker for the Quick Cook or Regular cycle. Place the butter in the rice cooker bowl. When the butter is melted, add the fennel seeds and bulgur; stir to coat and thoroughly heat the grains, 3 to 4 minutes; the bulgur should smell toasty.

2. Add the water and a few pinches of salt. Add the fresh and dried cherries. Stir just to combine, close the cover, and reset for the Regular cycle or let the Regular cycle complete.

3. When the machine switches to the Keep Warm cycle, lay a double layer of paper towels inside on top of the bulgur. Close the cover and let the pilaf steam for 15 minutes. Discard the paper towels and gently fluff the pilaf with a wooden or plastic rice paddle or wooden spoon. This dish will hold for 1 hour on Keep Warm. To serve, mound into a wide bowl or onto a small heated platter, and serve with a dollop of the yogurt or sprinkled with the feta. Serve hot.

1 tablespoon (14 g) butter

1 teaspoon fennel seeds or aniseed, ground in a mortar and pestle

1⅓ cups (229 g) medium or coarse bulgur

2¼ cups (530 ml) water

Salt

4 to 5 ounces (115 to 140 g) fresh Bing cherries, pitted and halved, or frozen pitted Bing cherries, thawed and halved

¼ cup (40 g) dried tart cherries

1 cup (230 g) plain Greek yogurt or ⅓ cup (50 g) crumbled feta cheese, for serving (optional)

1 tablespoon (14 g) unsalted butter

1 tablespoon (10 g) minced shallots

2 tablespoons (15 g) minced celery

1½ cups (355 ml) chicken stock

1 cup (150 g) fresh peas

½ teaspoon salt

½ cup (93 g) long-grain white rice

½ cup (90 g) Italian Arborio or California medium-grain rice

RICE PILAF WITH FRESH PEAS

MACHINE: Medium (6-cup [990 g]) rice cooker; fuzzy logic or on/off

CYCLE: Quick Cook and/or Regular

SERVES: 3 to 4

Rice has a natural affinity for peas. Food writer Bert Greene once remarked that fresh peas in the pod will eventually be as rare and as expensive as truffles. With due respect, this wonderful recipe should be made exclusively when fresh peas hit the market; frozen peas just will not taste the same. This recipe is made with two different rices, to give the pilaf a firmer texture than if it was made with all medium-grain rice, which is stickier.

1. Set the rice cooker for the Quick Cook or Regular cycle. Place the butter in the rice cooker bowl. When melted, add the shallots and celery. Cook, stirring a few times, until softened, about 2 minutes. Add the stock, peas, salt, and rices; stir just to combine. Close the cover and reset for the Regular cycle or let the Regular cycle complete.

2. When the machine switches to the Keep Warm cycle, let the rice steam for 10 minutes. Fluff with a wooden or plastic rice paddle or wooden spoon. This pilaf will hold on Keep Warm for up to 1 hour. Serve hot.

LEMON BASMATI PILAF

MACHINE: Medium (6-cup [990 g]) rice cooker; fuzzy logic or on/off

CYCLE: Regular

SERVES: 6

This is a wonderful accompaniment to just about any type of meal, from a mixed vegetable curry to barbecued meat and poultry. Please use an organic lemon if you can. You can pick out the whole spices and discard them before serving, or portion the rice with them still in there.

....

1. Place the rice in a fine strainer or bowl, rinse with cold water until the water runs clear, and drain.

2. Place the rice in the rice cooker bowl. Add the broth, lemon juice and zest, and salt; swirl just to combine. Toss in the cardamom pods or ginger. Close the cover and set for the Regular cycle.

3. When the machine switches to the Keep Warm cycle, let the rice steam for 15 minutes. Fluff the rice with a wooden or plastic rice paddle or wooden spoon. This rice will hold for 2 hours on Keep Warm. Serve hot.

2 cups (380 g) white basmati rice

2½ cups (590 ml) chicken broth

Juice and grated zest of 1 lemon

Pinch of sea salt

4 green cardamom pods, lightly cracked, or 2 slices fresh ginger (you can leave the peel on)

Juice of 1 lemon

8 baby artichokes of equal size

2 cups (360 g) Arborio or other medium-grain (risotto-style) rice

½ stick (¼ cup [55 g]) unsalted butter, cut into 8 pieces

2 medium-size shallots, minced

¼ cup (15 g) minced fresh Italian parsley leaves

3 cups (705 ml) chicken stock

½ teaspoon salt

Freshly ground black pepper

3 tablespoons (15 g) freshly grated Parmesan cheese, plus more for serving

BABY ARTICHOKES AND ARBORIO RICE

MACHINE: Medium (6-cup [990 g]) or large (10-cup [1.7 kg]) rice cooker; fuzzy logic or on/off

CYCLE: Regular

SERVES: 4

In the Puglia area of Italy, rice is cooked "Spanish" style—that is, similar to paella. Called a *tiella*, after the round terra-cotta dish it is baked in, the rice is layered with vegetables. You can use other Italian medium-grain rices in this dish, such as the Argentinean-grown Carnaroli rice imported by Lotus Foods.

....

1. Fill a large bowl with cold water and pour the lemon juice into it. Prepare the artichokes by bending the outer leaves back and snapping them off until only the yellow inside leaves remain. You will remove more leaves than you think you should; this is okay. How many you remove will depend on the size and tenderness of each artichoke. Cut ½ inch (1.3 cm) off the top of each artichoke with a sharp paring knife and trim the bottoms flat. Cut each in half lengthwise. Place the artichokes in the lemon water as you work to prevent discoloration.

2. Place the rice in a fine strainer or bowl, rinse with cold water until the water runs clear, and drain.

3. Place the butter pieces evenly over the bottom of the rice cooker bowl. Sprinkle with the shallots, then cover with the rice, then the parsley. Arrange the artichoke halves on top, stem sides slightly down, pressing into the rice. Pour the stock over the layered ingredients. Close the cover and set for the Regular cycle.

4. When the machine switches to the Keep Warm cycle, stir in the salt, pepper to taste, and cheese. Close the cooker and let the rice steam for 10 minutes.

5. Serve immediately. Spoon the rice and vegetables onto serving plates and pass more cheese on the side.

BUTTERNUT SQUASH RISOTTO

MACHINE: Medium (6-cup [990 g]) or large (10-cup [1.7 kg]) rice cooker; fuzzy logic or on/off

CYCLE: Quick Cook and/or Regular or Porridge

SERVES: 4 to 5

This risotto is heavier on the vegetables (the winter squash and the onion) than is traditional, but it is a favorite autumn and winter variation. Use less squash if you like, but the extra amount contributes a lovely flavor and color along with a nutritional boost. You can also use half stock and half water in order not to overwhelm the delicate squash flavor. You can add some diced zucchini as well; it is a good flavor combination. The unconventional addition of lime juice brightens the flavor of the squash.

....

1. Set the rice cooker for the Quick Cook or Regular cycle. Place the olive oil and butter in the rice cooker bowl. When the butter melts, add the onion. Cook, stirring a few times, until softened, about 2 minutes. Add the rice and stir with a wooden or plastic rice paddle or wooden spoon to coat the grains with the hot butter. Cook, stirring a few times, until the grains of rice are transparent except for a white spot on each, 3 to 5 minutes. Add the squash, water, and stock; stir to combine. Close the cover and reset for the Porridge cycle, or for the Regular cycle and set a timer for 20 minutes.

2. When the machine switches to the Keep Warm cycle or the timer sounds, stir the risotto. It should be only a bit liquid, and the rice should be al dente, tender with just a touch of tooth resistance. If needed, cook for a few minutes longer. This risotto will hold on Keep Warm for up to 1 hour.

3. When ready to serve, add the butter. Close the cover for a minute to let the butter melt. Stir in the lime juice, parsley, cheese, and salt to taste. Serve immediately.

2 tablespoons (30 ml) olive oil

2 tablespoons (28 g) unsalted butter

⅔ cup (110 g) finely chopped yellow onion

1 cup (180 g) plus 2 tablespoons (23 g) medium-grain risotto rice (*superfino* Arborio, Carnaroli, or Vialone nano)

1¾ to 2 cups (245 to 280 g) peeled and seeded butternut squash cut into ½-inch (1.3 cm) cubes

1½ cups (355 ml) water

1½ cups (355 ml) chicken, veal, or vegetable stock

TO FINISH

2 teaspoons unsalted butter

2 tablespoons (30 ml) fresh lime juice

¼ cup (15 g) minced fresh Italian parsley leaves

¼ cup (25 g) freshly grated Parmesan cheese, plus more for serving

Salt

3 cups (705 ml) chicken stock, or 1 can (14.5 ounces, or 410 g) chicken broth plus water to equal 3 cups (705 ml)

Pinch of saffron threads

1 tablespoon (15 ml) olive oil

1 tablespoon (14 g) unsalted butter

¾ cup (120 g) finely chopped yellow onion

¼ cup (60 ml) dry white wine

1 cup (180 g) plus 2 tablespoons (42 g) medium-grain risotto rice (*superfino* Arborio, Carnaroli, or Vialone nano)

TO FINISH

1 tablespoon (14 g) unsalted butter

¼ cup (25 g) freshly grated Parmesan cheese, plus more for serving

Salt

RISOTTO MILANESE

MACHINE: Medium (6-cup [990 g]) or large (10-cup [1.7 kg]) rice cooker; fuzzy logic or on/off

CYCLE: Quick Cook and/or Regular or Porridge

SERVES: 4 to 5

Risotto Milanese, or risotto with saffron, is the national dish of the Lombardy region of Italy. It has been made there since the late eighteenth century as a special first course washed down with red wine. Use saffron threads here, as powdered saffron is really a lot more potent; you want a faint saffron flavor, not overpowering. It is traditionally served as a starchy side dish to osso bucco (braised veal shanks) and *carbonata* (Milanese beef stew).

....

1. In a small saucepan or in the microwave, heat 1 cup (235 ml) of the stock and crush the saffron into it; let stand for 15 minutes.

2. Set the rice cooker for the Quick Cook or Regular cycle. Place the olive oil and butter in the rice cooker bowl. When the butter melts, add the onion. Cook, stirring a few times, until softened, about 2 minutes. Stir in the wine and cook for 1 minute. Add the rice and stir occasionally until the grains are transparent except for a white spot on each, 3 to 5 minutes. Stir in the saffron stock and remaining 2 cups (470 ml) chicken stock. Close the cover and reset for the Porridge cycle, or for the Regular cycle and set a timer for 20 minutes.

3. When the machine switches to the Keep Warm cycle or the timer sounds, stir the rice with a wooden or plastic rice paddle or wooden spoon. The risotto should be only a bit liquid and the rice should be al dente, tender with just a touch of tooth resistance. If needed, cook for a few minutes longer. This risotto will hold on Keep Warm for up to 1 hour.

4. When ready to serve, add the butter. Close the cover for a minute to let the butter melt. Stir in the cheese and salt to taste. Serve immediately.

RICE COOKER PAELLA

MACHINE: Large (10-cup [1.7 kg]) rice cooker; fuzzy logic or on/off

CYCLE: Quick Cook and/or Regular

SERVES: 8

You will need a large (10-cup [1.7 kg]) rice cooker to prepare paella for 8; halve the recipe for medium (6-cup [990 g]) machines. Don't be tempted to make this without the saffron; it is essential. You can order it (rather) reasonably from Penzeys, the spice merchants.

....

1. In a small nonstick skillet, heat 1 tablespoon (15 ml) of the olive oil over medium-high heat. When hot, add the chicken and cook, stirring, until just cooked through, 5 to 7 minutes. Remove the skillet from the heat.

2. Set the rice cooker for the Quick Cook or Regular cycle. Add the remaining 3 tablespoons (45 ml) of olive oil to the rice cooker bowl. When hot, add the onion. Cook, stirring a few times, until softened, about 2 minutes. Add the garlic, bell pepper, and tomatoes, stir to combine, and close the cover. Cook, stirring a few times, until the tomatoes break down and the bell pepper softens, about 10 minutes. Add the sausage, calamari, rice, chicken, water, salt, and black pepper; stir to combine. A pinch at a time, crumble the saffron threads into the rice bowl. Close the cover and reset for the Regular cycle or let the Regular cycle complete. When the liquid boils (open the cooker occasionally to check, if yours doesn't have a glass lid), add the green beans, stir quickly to combine, and close again.

3. When the machine switches to the Keep Warm cycle, be ready to act quickly. Open the cover, toss in the scallops, and quickly stir them into the rice mixture. Place the shrimp around the border of the rice cooker bowl, pressing them partway into the rice, so that their tails stick up. Sprinkle the peas over the entire surface of the rice. Nestle the clams about halfway into the rice, hinged sides down. Close the cover and let the paella steam until the clams open and the shrimp turn pink, about 15 minutes. Serve the paella immediately.

¼ cup (60 ml) extra-virgin olive oil, divided

2 boneless, skinless chicken thighs, trimmed of fat and cut into ¾-inch (1.9 cm) pieces

1 medium-size onion, chopped

2 cloves garlic, peeled

1 medium-size red bell pepper, seeded and cut into strips, the strips halved crosswise

1 cup (180 g) seeded and chopped fresh tomatoes

2 ounces (55 g) fully cooked smoked garlicky sausage (Spanish chorizo is traditional), sliced ⅓-inch (8 mm) thick

4 calamari, cleaned, bodies cut into ⅓-inch (8 mm)-wide rings, and each set of tentacles halved

3 cups (540 g) Arborio, Valencia, or other medium-grain white rice (not Japanese style)

5 cups (1.2 L) water

2 teaspoons salt

½ teaspoon freshly ground black pepper

½ teaspoon saffron threads

1 cup (100 g) fresh green beans, ends trimmed, cut into 1½-inch (3.8 cm) lengths

½ cup (65 g) small scallops

8 medium-size or large shrimp, shelled (tails left on) and deveined

½ cup (65 g) frozen peas

8 small clams, washed in cold water to remove sand

NOTE

If the clams do not open, perhaps there is not enough heat remaining in the rice cooker. Take them out and put them in a medium-size saucepan with about 1 inch (2.5 cm) of water. Cover the pot and bring the water to a boil. The clams should open in a few minutes. Throw out any that do not.

6

STEAMED DINNERS

Steamed Chicken Breasts with Warm Mango Sauce
and Coconut Rice 96
Steamed Salmon Steaks with Pineapple Salsa 99
Steamed Ginger Salmon and Asparagus in Black Bean Sauce 100
Steamed Halibut Steaks and Scallops with Sweet Red Pepper Sauce.... 102
Steamed Shrimp and Jasmine Rice... 104
Steamed Sausages and Sauerkraut with Champagne 107

STEAMED CHICKEN BREASTS WITH WARM MANGO SAUCE AND COCONUT RICE

MACHINE: Large (10-cup [1.7 kg]) rice cooker; on/off only

CYCLE: Regular

SERVES: 4

This dish combines tropical mangos with steamed chicken breasts. Serve this dish from the steamer baskets with coconut rice and steamed asparagus and/or chayote squash, a vegetable that often is served steamed or sautéed as a side vegetable in Mexico.

1. Rinse the rice in a fine strainer until the water runs clear. Place the rice in the rice cooker bowl. Add the coconut milk, water, and salt, if using; swirl to combine.

2. Coat the steamer baskets with nonstick cooking spray and arrange the chicken in one basket. Place the asparagus and/or chayote in the other basket or arrange it around the chicken. Place the steamer baskets in the rice cooker. Close the cover and set for the Regular cycle.

3. Make the Warm Mango Sauce: In a medium-size saucepan, combine the mango, wine, vinegar, sugar, ginger, and allspice. Bring to a boil over medium heat, stirring to dissolve the sugar. Reduce the heat to low and simmer, uncovered, for 5 minutes. Remove from the heat and set aside.

4. When the machine switches to the Keep Warm cycle, check to make sure the chicken is no longer pink inside and the vegetables are tender. Fluff the rice with a wooden or plastic rice paddle or wooden spoon.

5. To serve, transfer the rice to a serving platter and top with the chicken. Arrange the vegetables around the rice and season with salt and pepper to taste. Reheat the Warm Mango Sauce and spoon a small amount over the chicken. Garnish with cilantro. Pass the remaining Warm Mango Sauce at the table.

2½ cups (450 g) basmati rice or other aromatic long-grain rice, such as jasmine or Jasmati

2 cans (14 ounces, or 410 g each) unsweetened coconut milk (can be light)

¼ cup (60 ml) water

⅛ teaspoon salt (optional)

4 boneless, skinless chicken breast halves

1 pound (455 g) thick asparagus spears, tough bottoms discarded, and/or 2 chayote squashes, peeled, seeded, halved, and cut into 1½-inch (3.8 cm)-thick slices

WARM MANGO SAUCE

1 large ripe mango, peeled, seeded, and cut into neat ½-inch (1.3 cm) pieces

¼ cup (60 ml) dry white wine

2 tablespoons (30 ml) rice vinegar

2 tablespoons (26 g) sugar

2 teaspoons peeled and minced fresh ginger

⅛ teaspoon ground allspice

Salt

Freshly ground black pepper

3 tablespoons (3 g) minced fresh cilantro leaves, for garnish

MARINADE AND SALMON

¾ cup (175 ml) dry sake

¾ cup (175 ml) reduced-sodium soy sauce

⅓ cup (67 g) sugar

4 salmon steaks (6 to 8 ounces, or 170 to 225 g), ¾ inch (1.9 cm) thick

PINEAPPLE SALSA

1½ cups (235 g) diced fresh pineapple

⅓ cup (100 g) seeded and minced red bell pepper

¼ cup (40 g) minced red onion

¼ cup (4 g) minced fresh cilantro leaves

Juice and grated zest of 1 large lime

2½ teaspoons seeded and minced jalapeño chile

2 to 3 large chard leaves, stems discarded, or Napa cabbage leaves, for lining steamer basket (optional)

STEAMED SALMON STEAKS WITH PINEAPPLE SALSA

MACHINE: Large (10-cup [1.7 kg]) rice cooker; on/off only

CYCLE: Regular

SERVES: 4

Salmon steaks, now readily available because of farm-raised fish, are a sure thing for a fast dinner. This marinade is wonderful. Serve with some hot jasmine rice.

....

1. Make the marinade: Place the marinade ingredients in a shallow bowl; whisk to combine. Place the salmon in the marinade, coating both sides well. Cover and refrigerate for 1 to 2 hours, turning once.

2. Make the Pineapple Salsa: Place the salsa ingredients in a small bowl; stir to combine. Cover and refrigerate until serving.

3. Fill the rice cooker bowl one-quarter full of hot water, close the cover, and set for the Regular cycle.

4. Line the two steamer baskets with a single layer of chard or cabbage leaves or a piece of parchment paper. Remove the salmon steaks from the marinade and arrange on one or two tiers of the steamer baskets. (If you are steaming vegetables with the salmon, you can arrange them around the sides of the tiers.) When the water comes to a boil, place the steamer baskets in the cooker and close the cover. Set a timer and steam for 18 to 23 minutes. Check for doneness; the fish should be opaque and firm.

5. Serve the salmon immediately, with the Pineapple Salsa.

STEAMED GINGER SALMON AND ASPARAGUS IN BLACK BEAN SAUCE

MACHINE: Large (10-cup [1.7 kg]) rice cooker; on/off only

CYCLE: Regular

SERVES: 3 to 4

A full Asian-style meal in the rice cooker! The rice is cooked below while the salmon and asparagus steam above.

....

1. Rinse the rice, if desired. Place in the rice cooker with the water; add 3 cups (705 ml) water for Japanese-style rice, 3¼ cups (765 ml) for domestic.

2. Make the sauce. In a small bowl, stir together the black bean garlic sauce, sake, and sugar. Place the asparagus in a medium-size bowl and toss with half of the sauce.

3. Line the steamer basket with a single layer of chard, cabbage, or lettuce leaves. Place the salmon in the center of the basket. Cut six slits in the fish; insert a ginger slice into each slit. Spread the remaining sauce over the fish. Arrange the asparagus around the fish. Place the steamer basket in the rice cooker. Close the cover and set for the Regular cycle.

4. When the machine switches to the Keep Warm cycle, let steam for 10 minutes. Check for doneness; the salmon and asparagus should be cooked through. If not, cover again and allow the fish to finish cooking, checking at 10-minute intervals.

5. Garnish with the green onions and serve.

2¼ cups (337 g) (3 rice cooker cups) Japanese-style or domestic medium-grain white jasmine rice

3 or 3¼ cups (705 or 765 ml) water (see directions)

BLACK BEAN SAUCE

2 tablespoons (28 g) black bean garlic sauce (available in Asian markets or well-stocked supermarkets)

2 teaspoons sake

1 teaspoon sugar

1 pound (455 g) fresh asparagus, bottoms snapped off and stalks cut on the diagonal into 1½-inch (3.8 cm)-long pieces

2 to 3 large chard leaves, stems discarded, Napa cabbage leaves, or lettuce leaves, for lining steamer basket

One ¾- to 1-pound (340 to 455 g) salmon fillet, rinsed and patted dry

6 thin slices peeled fresh ginger

2 green onions, white and tender green parts, slivered, for garnish

STEAMED HALIBUT STEAKS AND SCALLOPS WITH SWEET RED PEPPER SAUCE

MACHINE: Large (10-cup [1.7 kg]) rice cooker; on/off only

CYCLE: Regular

SERVES: 4

This red pepper sauce is delightful on the halibut (it is also good on lingcod) and scallops. Try using Della long-grain white rice here.

....

1. Rinse and pat dry the halibut and scallops. Place on a plate and sprinkle with the oil, salt and pepper to taste, and the wine. Refrigerate while preparing the rice. Place the rice in the rice cooker bowl. Add the water and salt; swirl to combine.

2. Line the two steamer baskets with a single layer of chard or cabbage leaves or a sheet of parchment paper. Arrange the fish on two tiers (2 steaks per basket) of the steamer baskets in a single layer and top with the thyme sprigs. Loosely arrange the green beans around the outside of the steaks. Place the steaming baskets in the rice cooker. Close the cover and set for the Regular cycle.

3. Make the sauce. Combine the peppers and onions with the oil in a sauté pan over medium heat. Cook until soft, 5 to 10 minutes. Add the vinegar, thyme, and cayenne. Transfer the mixture to a food processor and process until smooth. Add the sour cream and pulse to combine. Season with salt and pepper to taste. Transfer the sauce to a saucepan and keep warm until serving.

Four 6- to 8-ounce (170 to 225 g) halibut steaks (1 inch [2.5 cm] thick)

¾ to 1 pound (340 to 455 g) large scallops

2 tablespoons (30 ml) olive oil

Salt

Freshly ground black pepper

2 tablespoons (30 ml) dry white wine

1¾ cups (350 g) domestic aromatic long-grain rice, such as Della or Jasmati

2¾ cups (645 ml) water

Pinch of salt

2 to 3 large chard leaves, stems discarded, or Napa cabbage leaves, for lining steamer basket (optional)

4 sprigs fresh thyme

1 pound (455 g) fresh green beans, ends trimmed

SWEET RED PEPPER SAUCE

4 large red bell peppers, seeded and cut into pieces

2 large yellow onions, chopped

3 to 4 tablespoons (45 to 60 ml) olive oil

3 tablespoons (45 ml) balsamic vinegar

Pinch of fresh or dried thyme leaves

Pinch of cayenne pepper

⅓ cup (77 g) sour cream or (73 g) crème fraîche

Salt

Freshly ground black pepper

4. When the machine switches to the Keep Warm cycle, let steam for 10 minutes. Check for doneness: The halibut and scallops should be opaque and firm to the touch, and the vegetables should be cooked through. Fluff the rice with a wooden or plastic rice paddle or wooden spoon.

5. To serve, divide the fish, rice, and beans among four dinner plates and pass the sauce at the table.

STEAMED SHRIMP AND JASMINE RICE

MACHINE: Medium (6-cup [990 g]) or large (10-cup [1.7 kg]) rice cooker; on/off only

CYCLE: Regular

SERVES: 4

Shrimp is an excellent seafood for the rice cooker because it cooks so quickly. If your cooker has a glass lid, it's easy to tell when the shrimp are cooked by their bright orange-pink color; if you have to lift the lid to check the shrimp, do so with care to avoid the steam. If the shrimp is finished before the end of the rice cooking cycle, carefully remove the shrimp and green onions, either by removing the whole steaming tray or by transferring the ingredients with a spatula or tongs.

Timing this recipe takes a little practice, but the whole dish couldn't be easier. Chopping up and mixing in the steamed green onions gives great flavor and texture to the cooked rice. You might try this with baby leeks instead of green onions. This is a light meal, suitable for lunch or Sunday night supper.

....

1⅓ cups (240 g) Thai jasmine rice

2⅔ cups (630 ml) water

Pinch of salt

8 green onions, trimmed to fit steaming tray

1 pound (455 g) medium-size shrimp, shelled (tails left on) and deveined

2 pinches of dillweed

Ground white pepper

Sprigs of fresh Italian parsley, basil, or sage, for garnish

1. Rinse the rice. Place it in the rice cooker bowl with the water and salt; swirl to combine. Close the cover and set for the Regular cycle.

2. Place the green onions on the steamer tray and lay the shrimp on top in a single layer. Sprinkle with the dillweed and white pepper to season.

3. About 8 minutes before the end of the Regular cycle (depending on brand and size, about 15 minutes into the cycle), place the steaming tray in the cooker and close the cover. Steam the shrimp for about 6 minutes, until the color has changed to orange-pink. Do not overcook the shrimp, or they will become tough. Remove the steaming tray and place the shrimp in a warm covered dish. Let the green onions cool, then chop them enough to stir them into the rice when it is done; you will have about ⅓ cup (33 g).

4. When the machine switches to the Keep Warm cycle, stir the green onions into the rice with a plastic or wooden rice paddle or wooden spoon.

5. To serve, mound the rice on a serving platter or four individual plates, place the shrimp on top, and garnish with the herb sprigs.

2½ to 3 pounds (1.1 to 1.4 kg) sauerkraut, rinsed

⅓ cup (80 ml) dry champagne or sparkling white wine

8 fully cooked sausages, such as smoked chicken-apple or bockwurst with chives

12 medium-size red or white new potatoes, cut in half or quarters, or 24 baby creamer potatoes, left whole and unpeeled

½ stick (¼ cup [55 g]) unsalted butter, for serving

2 teaspoons dillweed, for serving

STEAMED SAUSAGES AND SAUERKRAUT WITH CHAMPAGNE

MACHINE: Large (10-cup [1.7 kg]) rice cooker; on/off only

CYCLE: Regular

SERVES: 4

With the advent of the healthier sausages, it is now easy to eat them once a week. Here is an incredibly easy entrée. The amount of sauerkraut depends on your diners; anyone from Europe will eat a hearty serving. You can brown the sausages first in a skillet if you like, but that is optional. Serve with a variety of mustards and some butter and dillweed on the potatoes.

1. Fill the rice cooker bowl one-quarter full of hot water, close the cover, and set for the Regular cycle.

2. Line two steamer baskets with a single sheet of parchment paper each. Divide the sauerkraut in half and arrange it like a bed in the center of both baskets; drizzle with the champagne. Place 4 sausages on each bed of sauerkraut, then loosely arrange the potatoes around the sauerkraut. When the water comes to a boil, place the baskets in the cooker and close the cover. Set a timer and steam for 30 to 40 minutes. Check for doneness: The potatoes should be tender when pierced with the tip of a knife and the sausages nice and hot.

3. Serve immediately, with each diner having 2 sausages, sauerkraut, and some potatoes with 1 tablespoon (14 g) butter and ½ teaspoon dillweed sprinkled on.

DESSERTS

Old-Fashioned Rice Pudding 110
Tres Leches Rice Pudding 113
Tapioca Pudding 114
English Pudding with Cranberries and Walnuts 117
Poached Rhubarb and Strawberries 118
Steamed Cappuccino Custards 121
Steamed Chocolate Custards 122

OLD-FASHIONED RICE PUDDING

MACHINE: Medium (6-cup [990 g]) rice cooker; fuzzy logic only

CYCLE: Porridge

SERVES: 6

Here is the quintessential rice pudding of everyone's childhood. It is sweet and creamy, no fancy or exotic ingredients. Whole milk is best, but 2 percent works fine. It is slowly simmered in the rice cooker and ready to eat as soon as it cools. Remember that rice pudding thickens considerably when chilled as the starch in the rice sets up.

⅔ cup (130 g) medium-grain white rice, such as Arborio, Calriso, or other California-grown rice

4 cups (940 ml) milk

1 large egg

⅓ cup (67 g) sugar

1 teaspoon pure vanilla extract

½ teaspoon cinnamon

....

1. Place the rice and milk in the rice cooker bowl; stir to combine. Close the cover and set for the Porridge cycle.

2. When the machine switches to the Keep Warm cycle, combine the egg, sugar, and vanilla in a small bowl and beat with a whisk. Open the rice cooker, spoon a few tablespoons (45 to 60 ml) of the rice milk into the egg mixture, and beat with a wooden spoon. Beating the rice milk constantly, pour the rest of the egg mixture into the rice cooker bowl. Stir for a minute to combine. Close the cover and reset for a second Porridge cycle. Stir every 15 to 20 minutes until the desired thickness is reached.

3. Pour the pudding into six cups. Sprinkle cinnamon on top. Serve warm or let cool slightly and refrigerate for at least 1 hour. When cold, cover with plastic wrap and store for up to 4 days.

1½ cups (270 g) Arborio rice or other short-grain rice (see headnote)

2 cups (470 ml) water

½ teaspoon salt

½ cup (120 ml) evaporated milk

⅔ cup (160 ml) unsweetened coconut milk (Don't shake the can; use the top cream.)

1 cup (235 ml) sweetened condensed milk, organic preferred

1½ teaspoons pure vanilla extract

½ teaspoon freshly grated nutmeg

1 cinnamon stick

1 strip (3 to 4 inches, or 7.5 to 10 cm) of lemon zest (Cut around the whole lemon for one long, wide strip.)

TRES LECHES RICE PUDDING

MACHINE: Medium (6-cup [990 g]) rice cooker; fuzzy logic or on/off

CYCLE: Regular and/or Porridge

SERVES: 4

You can make this egg-free rice pudding with a number of glutinous rices, such as Italian Arborio, Vialono nano, Japanese Tamaki *haiga mai*, Lundberg Sweet Brown Rice, or a black rice like Chinese Forbidden Rice or Italian *riso nero* (the hybrid of Arborio and Forbidden rice grown in northern Italy). Serve with whipped cream.

1. Place the rice in a fine strainer or bowl, and rinse with cold water until the water runs clear.

2. Place the rice, water, and salt in the rice cooker bowl. Close the cover and set for the Regular cycle.

3. When the machine switches to the Keep Warm cycle, stir in the evaporated, coconut, and condensed milks, vanilla, and nutmeg. Submerge the cinnamon stick and lemon zest. Reset for the Porridge cycle. (If the cycle doesn't start immediately, disconnect the cord from the outlet, let stand 15 minutes, then plug back in and reset the cycle.)

4. When the machine switches to the Keep Warm cycle for a second time, open the cover and let the pudding cool at room temperature, uncovered, for about 20 minutes, stirring occasionally to prevent a skin from forming on the surface. Discard the cinnamon stick and zest strip. Serve warm or transfer to a covered glass bowl and refrigerate until chilled.

TAPIOCA PUDDING

MACHINE: Medium (6-cup [990 g]) rice cooker; fuzzy logic only

CYCLE: Porridge

SERVES: 3 to 4

This pudding uses the whole pearl tapioca, a food that most Western cooks have never used, but it is a staple in tropical countries where flour would clump and spoil in short order. The flavor of this made-from-scratch pudding trounces that of ready-made or packaged tapioca mixes. If desired, fold in fresh or frozen berries, sliced peaches or mangos, poached pears, or other fruit, and top with whipped cream.

....

1. Place the tapioca in the rice cooker bowl. In a 4-cup (940 ml) measuring cup or small bowl, whisk together the milk, egg, sugar, and salt. Pour the milk mixture over the tapioca; stir to combine. Close the cover and set for the Porridge cycle.

2. When the machine switches to the Keep Warm cycle, remove the bowl from the cooker and stir in the vanilla. Pour the pudding into a large bowl or individual dessert dishes. Let cool. Serve warm, if desired, or refrigerate, covered with plastic wrap.

3 tablespoons (33 g) small pearl tapioca (not minute or instant tapioca)

2 cups (470 ml) milk (low-fat or nonfat is fine)

1 large egg

½ cup (100 g) sugar

Pinch of salt

1 teaspoon pure vanilla extract

½ cup (120 ml) hot water

½ cup (170 g) light molasses

2 teaspoons baking soda

¼ teaspoon salt

¼ teaspoon ground ginger

¼ teaspoon ground cinnamon

1½ cups (188 g)
all-purpose flour

2 cups (200 g) fresh or
(220 g) frozen (and thawed)
cranberries

½ cup (60 g) chopped walnuts

Custard sauce (optional)

ENGLISH PUDDING WITH CRANBERRIES AND WALNUTS

MACHINE: Large (10-cup [1.7 kg]) rice cooker; on/off only

CYCLE: Regular

SERVES: 8 to 10

This is an Americanized version of the very traditional, very beloved English pudding called *spotted dick*, which originally called for shredded suet and raisins. Serve with a package of Bird's custard sauce made according to the package instructions, if you want to be very English.

1. Set up the rice cooker for steaming by placing a small trivet or wire cooling rack in the bottom of the rice bowl. Fill the bowl one-quarter to one-third full of hot water, close the cover, and set for the Regular cycle. Generously grease or coat the inside of a 1½-quart (6-cup, or 1.4 L) round melon-shaped tin pudding mold with a clip-on lid with butter-flavored nonstick cooking spray.

2. In a large bowl, combine all the ingredients (except the custard sauce) in the order given with a large rubber spatula. Stir well with a folding motion until evenly moistened.

3. Scrape the batter into the prepared mold, filling it two-thirds full; snap on the lid. Set the mold on the trivet or wire rack in the bottom of the cooker, making sure it is centered and not tipped. Close the cover and reset the cooker for the Regular cycle to bring back to a rolling boil, if necessary. Set a timer and steam for 1 hour, checking a few times to be sure the water doesn't boil off. Check the pudding for doneness; it should feel slightly firm to the touch, yet slightly moist. It should be puffed, rising to fill the mold, and a cake tester inserted in the center should come out clean. Unplug the machine to turn it off.

4. Using oven mitts, carefully transfer the mold from the steamer to a wire rack and remove the lid. Let stand for a few minutes, then turn upside down to unmold the pudding onto the rack or a serving plate.

5. Cut into wedges and serve with custard sauce, if you like.

POACHED RHUBARB AND STRAWBERRIES

MACHINE: Large (10-cup [1.7 kg]) rice cooker; fuzzy logic only

CYCLE: Porridge

MAKES: About 4 cups (640 g)

Don't have time to make a strawberry-rhubarb pie? Well, this early-summer fresh fruit compote has all the flavor and pretty color without any of the fuss. Note that the recipe says to be careful with the stirring so that the fruits do not get stringy and mushy. The flavor is so very delightful and especially good with vanilla gelato.

....

1. Place the water, sugar, vanilla bean, and rhubarb in the rice cooker bowl. Close the cover and set for the Porridge cycle. Set a timer for 30 minutes; when the timer sounds, add the strawberries and stir once to distribute. Close the cover and let the cycle complete.

2. When the machine switches to the Keep Warm cycle, carefully open the cover, remove the bowl from the cooker, and let cool. Do not stir. Serve the compote warm or at room temperature, or pour into a storage container, cover, and refrigerate overnight to serve chilled, ladled into dessert bowls. Keeps for up to 4 days in the refrigerator.

1 cup (235 ml) water

1 cup (200 g) sugar

1 vanilla bean, split

1 pound (455 g) fresh rhubarb stems, cut into 1½-inch (3.8 cm) chunks (about 4 cups [488 g])

1½ pints (510 g) fresh strawberries, rinsed, hulled, and halved

2 cups (470 ml) half-and-half

1½ tablespoons (9 g) instant espresso powder, such as Medaglia D'oro

6 large egg yolks

½ cup (100 g) sugar

Pinch of salt

STEAMED CAPPUCCINO CUSTARDS

MACHINE: Large (10-cup [1.7 kg]) rice cooker; on/off only

CYCLE: Regular

SERVES: 6

The unique, complex flavor of coffee is a natural infused into a cream mixture for this custard. This is a favorite!

1. Coat the inside of six custard cups or ramekins with butter-flavored nonstick cooking spray.

2. In a small saucepan, whisk together the half-and-half and espresso until smooth. Bring to a boil over medium heat, stirring occasionally. Remove from the heat.

3. In a medium-size bowl, gently whisk the egg yolks, sugar, and salt just until blended. Whisk the warm half-and-half into the mixture, beating with the whisk constantly to keep it from curdling. Pour the custard into the prepared custard cups. Cover each cup with a small square of aluminum foil and crimp the edges to seal airtight.

4. Add 4 cups (940 ml) hot water to the rice cooker bowl, close the cover, and set for the Regular cycle. When the water comes to a boil, arrange the cups in the tray or baskets (this works best steaming a double rack of custards at one time). Place the tray or baskets in the cooker and close the cover. Steam until the custards are just set and slightly wobbly in the center, 22 to 25 minutes. Unplug the machine to turn it off.

5. Remove each custard from the rice cooker with metal tongs. Remove the foil covers. Let cool, then serve at room temperature or refrigerate until ready to serve.

STEAMED CHOCOLATE CUSTARDS

MACHINE: Large (10-cup [1.7 kg]) rice cooker; on/off only

CYCLE: Regular

SERVES: 4

This is a delectable chocolate custard that begs for some whipped cream on top.

....

1. Coat the inside of four custard cups or ramekins with butter-flavored nonstick cooking spray.

2. In a small saucepan, whisk together the milk, chocolate chips, and cocoa over medium heat just until the chocolate melts, stirring occasionally.

3. In a medium-size bowl, combine the brown sugar and salt. Whisk in the whole egg, egg yolks, and vanilla until smooth. Whisk in about a quarter of the chocolate mixture, beating vigorously. Slowly pour in the remaining chocolate mixture in a steady stream, whisking constantly to avoid curdling. Pour the custard into the prepared custard cups. Cover each cup with a small square of aluminum foil and crimp the edges to seal airtight.

4. Add 4 cups (940 ml) of hot water to the rice cooker bowl, close the cover, and set for the Regular cycle. When the water comes to a boil, arrange the cups in the tray or baskets (this works best steaming a double rack of custards at one time). Place the tray or baskets in the cooker and close the cover. Steam until the custards are just set and slightly wobbly in the center, 35 to 40 minutes. Unplug the machine to turn it off.

5. Remove each custard from the rice cooker with metal tongs. Remove the foil covers. Let cool and then serve at room temperature or refrigerate until ready to serve.

1½ cups (355 ml) whole milk

½ cup (88 g) semisweet chocolate chips

2 tablespoons (10 g) Dutch-process unsweetened cocoa powder, such as Droste

¼ cup (60 g) firmly packed dark brown sugar

Pinch of salt

1 large egg

2 large egg yolks

½ teaspoon pure vanilla extract

INDEX

A

Almonds, in Wild Rice and Bulgur with Leeks and Toasted Almonds, 43
American Jasmine Rice, 7
American Long-Grain White Rice, 6
Aniseed, in Bulgur and Cherry Pilaf, 80
Apple Granola, 19
Apple (dried), in Apple Granola, 19
Arborio rice, 8
    Baby Artichokes and Arborio Rice, 87
    Butternut Squash Risotto, 88
    Old-Fashioned Rice Pudding, 110
    Rice Cooker Paella, 92–93
    Rice Pilaf with Fresh Peas, 83
    Risotto Milanese, 91
    Tres Leches Rice Pudding, 113
Artichokes, in Baby Artichokes and Arborio Rice, 87
Asparagus
    Steamed Chicken Breasts with Warm Mango Sauce and Coconut Rice, 96
    Steamed Ginger Salmon and Asparagus in Black Bean Sauce, 100

B

Baby Artichokes and Arborio Rice, 87
Barley grits, in Apple Granola, 19
Basil (fresh), in Rice with Fresh Greens for a Crowd, 33
Basmati rice
    Basmati Rice with Corn and Peas, 37
    Brown Basmati Rice, 9
    Greek Lemon and Dill Rice with Feta, 30
    Lemon Basmati Pilaf, 84
    recipe, 7
    Rice with Fresh Greens for a Crowd, 33
    Small-Batch Basmati Brown Rice, 8
    Steamed Chicken Breasts with Warm Mango Sauce and Coconut Rice, 96
Beans
    Frijoles Negros, 49
    Hummus, 50
    Italian White Beans, 46

Bell pepper(s)
    Frijoles Negros, 49
    Herbed Green Beans, 53
    Rice Cooker Paella, 92–93
    Steamed Halibut Steaks and Scallops with Sweet Red Pepper Sauce, 102–103
    Steamed Salmon Steaks with Pineapple Salsa, 99
Berries
    Poached Rhubarb and Strawberries, 118
    Sweet Breakfast Grits with Fresh Fruit, 22
    Vanilla Oatmeal Crème Brûlée with Berries, 16
Black Bean Sauce, Steamed Ginger Salmon and Asparagus in, 100
Black beans, in Frijoles Negros, 49
Black Japonica Rice, 9
Black Rice, 9
Broccoli florets, in Broccoli with Lemon Sauce, 53
Brown rice
    Brown Basmati Rice, 9
    Brown Jasmine Rice, 9
    Long- or Medium-Grain Brown Rice, 8
    Short-Grain Brown Rice, 8
    Small-Batch Basmati Brown Rice, 8
Bulgur cracked wheat
    Bulgur and Cherry Pilaf, 80
    Wild Rice and Bulgur with Leeks and Toasted Almonds, 43
Butternut squash, in Butternut Squash Risotto, 88

C

Cabbage, in Thanksgiving Jook, 26–27. See also Napa cabbage leaves
Calamari, in Rice Cooker Paella, 92–93
California medium-grain rice
    Old-Fashioned Rice Pudding, 110
    Rice Pilaf with Fresh Peas, 83
Cannellini beans, in Italian White Beans, 46
Cardamom pods, in Lemon Basmati Pilaf, 84
Carnaroli rice, 8
    Butternut Squash Risotto, 88
    Risotto Milanese, 91

Carolina rice
    Greek Lemon and Dill Rice with Feta, 30
    Rice with Fresh Greens for a Crowd, 33
Carrots
    Italian White Beans, 46
    Thanksgiving Jook, 26–27
Celery
    Herbed Green Beans, 53
    Italian White Beans, 46
    Rice Pilaf with Fresh Peas, 83
Champagne, in Steamed Sausages and Sauerkraut with Champagne, 107
Chard leaves
    Steamed Ginger Salmon and Asparagus in Black Bean Sauce, 100
    Steamed Halibut Steaks and Scallops with Sweet Red Pepper Sauce, 102–103
    Steamed Salmon Steaks with Pineapple Salsa, 99
Cheese. See Feta cheese; Parmesan cheese
Cherries (dried)
    Apple Granola, 19
    Bulgur and Cherry Pilaf, 80
    Maple-Cinnamon Rice Pudding, 21
Chicken
    Indonesian Rice Bowl, 40–41
    Rice Cooker Paella, 92–93
    Steamed Chicken Breasts with Warm Mango Sauce and Coconut Rice, 96
Chicken stock/broth
    Baby Artichokes and Arborio Rice, 87
    Butternut Squash Risotto, 88
    French Polenta, 74
    Greek Lemon and Dill Rice with Feta, 30
    Indonesian Rice Bowl, 40–41
    Italian White Beans, 46
    Lemon Basmati Pilaf, 84
    Rice Pilaf with Fresh Peas, 83
    Risotto Milanese, 91
    Wild Rice and Bulgur with Leeks and Toasted Almonds, 43
Chickpeas, in Hummus, 50
Chinese Sausage and Rice, 38
Chinese-Style Plain Rice, 7

Chives (fresh), in Shrimp and Grits, 66–67
Chocolate chips, in Steamed Chocolate
  Custards, 122
Cilantro
  Chinese Sausage and Rice, 38
  Steamed Chicken Breasts with Warm
    Mango Sauce and Coconut Rice, 96
  Steamed Salmon Steaks with Pineapple
    Salsa, 99
  Thanksgiving Jook, 26–27
Cinnamon stick, in Tres Leches Rice
  Pudding, 113
Clams, in Rice Cooker Paella, 92–93
Cocoa powder, in Steamed Chocolate
  Custards, 122
Coconut milk
  Steamed Chicken Breasts with Warm
    Mango Sauce and Coconut Rice, 96
  Tres Leches Rice Pudding, 113
Cool Whip, in Vanilla Oatmeal Crème Brûlée
  with Berries, 16
Corn
  Basmati Rice with Corn and Peas, 37
  Steamed Corn on the Cob, 57
Cracked rye or wheat
  Apple Granola, 19
  Wild Rice and Bulgur with Leeks and
    Toasted Almonds, 43
Cranberries
  Apple Granola, 19
  English Pudding with Cranberries and
    Walnuts, 117
  Maple-Cinnamon Rice Pudding, 21
Cream of Buckwheat cereal, in Apple
  Granola, 19
Creamy Breakfast Oatmeal, 12
Creamy Old-Fashioned Grits, 65
Creamy Traditional Grits, 62
Currants, in Apple Granola, 19
Custards
  Steamed Cappuccino Custards, 121
  Steamed Chocolate Custards, 122

D
Dates, in Creamy Breakfast Oatmeal, 12
Della rice, in Steamed Halibut Steaks and
  Scallops with Sweet Red Pepper
  Sauce, 102–103
Dill/dillweed
  Greek Lemon and Dill Rice with Feta, 30
  Steamed Sausages and Sauerkraut with
    Champagne, 107
  Steamed Shrimp and Jasmine Rice,
    104–105

E
Eggs
  Broccoli with Lemon Sauce, 53
  Old-Fashioned Rice Pudding, 110
  Steamed Chocolate Custards, 122
  Tapioca Pudding, 114
Egg yolks
  Steamed Cappuccino Custards, 121
  Steamed Chocolate Custards, 122
English Pudding with Cranberries and
  Walnuts, 117
Espresso powder, in Steamed Cappuccino
  Custards, 121
Evaporated milk, in Tres Leches Rice
  Pudding, 113

F
Fennel seeds, in Bulgur and Cherry Pilaf, 80
Feta cheese
  Bulgur and Cherry Pilaf, 80
  Greek Lemon and Dill Rice with Feta, 30
Fish and seafood
  Rice Cooker Paella, 92–93
  Shrimp and Grits, 66–67
  Steamed Ginger Salmon and Asparagus
    in Black Bean Sauce, 100
  Steamed Halibut Steaks and Scallops with
    Sweet Red Pepper Sauce, 102–103
  Steamed Salmon Steaks with Pineapple
    Salsa, 99
  Steamed Shrimp and Jasmine Rice,
    104–105
French Polenta, 74
Fresh Hominy, 70
Fried Grits, 69
Frijoles Negros, 49

G
Garlic
  Broccoli with Lemon Sauce, 53
  Hummus, 50
  Indonesian Rice Bowl, 40–41
  Rice Cooker Paella, 92–93
  Shrimp and Grits, 66–67
Ginger (fresh)
  Indonesian Rice Bowl, 40–41
  Lemon Basmati Pilaf, 84
  Spiced Yams with Ginger and Pears, 58
  Steamed Chicken Breasts with Warm
    Mango Sauce and Coconut Rice, 96
  Steamed Ginger Salmon and Asparagus
    in Black Bean Sauce, 100
  Thanksgiving Jook, 26–27
Granola, Hot Apple, 18–19
Greek Lemon and Dill Rice with Feta, 30
Greek yogurt
  Bulgur and Cherry Pilaf, 80
  Vanilla Oatmeal Crème Brûlée with
    Berries, 16
Green beans
  Herbed Green Beans, 53

Rice Cooker Paella, 92–93
  Steamed Halibut Steaks and Scallops with
    Sweet Red Pepper Sauce, 102–103
Green onions
  Chinese Sausage and Rice, 38
  Indonesian Rice Bowl, 40–41
  Steamed Ginger Salmon and Asparagus
    in Black Bean Sauce, 100
  Steamed Shrimp and Jasmine Rice,
    104–105
  Thanksgiving Jook, 26–27
Grits
  Creamy Old-Fashioned Grits, 65
  Creamy Traditional Grits, 62
  Fried Grits, 69
  Shrimp and Grits, 66–67
  Sweet Breakfast Grits with Fresh Fruit, 22
  Traditional Grits, 62

H
Half-and-half
  Steamed Cappuccino Custards, 121
  Vanilla Oatmeal Crème Brûlée with
    Berries, 16
Halibut Steaks and Scallops with Sweet Red
  Pepper Sauce, 102–103
Ham hock, in Italian White Beans, 46
Heavy cream
  Creamy Old-Fashioned Grits, 65
  Maple-Cinnamon Rice Pudding, 21
Herbed Green Beans, 54
Hominy, Fresh, 70
Honey, in Sweet Breakfast Grits with Fresh
  Fruit, 22
Hot Apple Granola, 18–19
Hummus, 50

I
Indonesian Rice Bowl, 40–41
Italian Polenta, 73
Italian White Beans, 46

J
Jalapeño chiles
  Frijoles Negros, 49
  Steamed Salmon Steaks with Pineapple
    Salsa, 99
Japanese White Rice with Umeboshi and
  Sesame, 34
Jasmati rice
  Greek Lemon and Dill Rice with Feta, 30
  Steamed Chicken Breasts with Warm
    Mango Sauce and Coconut Rice, 96
  Steamed Halibut Steaks and Scallops with
    Sweet Red Pepper Sauce, 102–103
Jasmine rice
  American Jasmine Rice, 7
  Brown Jasmine Rice, 9

Greek Lemon and Dill Rice with Feta, 30
Indonesian Rice Bowl, 40–41
Steamed Chicken Breasts with Warm
    Mango Sauce and Coconut Rice, 96
Steamed Ginger Salmon and Asparagus
    in Black Bean Sauce, 100
Steamed Shrimp and Jasmine Rice,
    104–105
Thai Jasmine Rice, 7
White Jasmine Blend, 7

L
Leeks, in Wild Rice and Bulgur with Leeks
    and Toasted Almonds, 43
Lemon Basmati Pilaf, 84
Lemon juice/zest
    Baby Artichokes and Arborio Rice, 87
    Broccoli with Lemon Sauce, 53
    Hummus, 50
    Lemon Basmati Pilaf, 84
    Shrimp and Grits, 66–67
    Tres Leches Rice Pudding, 113
Lettuce leaves, in Steamed Ginger Salmon
    and Asparagus in Black Bean Sauce,
    100
Lime juice
    Butternut Squash Risotto, 88
    Steamed Salmon Steaks with Pineapple
        Salsa, 99
Long-grain rice. See also Basmati rice;
    Jasmati rice; Jasmine rice
    American Long-Grain White Rice, 7
    Rice Pilaf with Fresh Peas, 83
Long- or Medium-Grain Brown Rice, 8

M
Mango, in Steamed Chicken Breasts with
    Warm Mango Sauce and Coconut
    Rice, 96
Maple-Cinnamon Rice Pudding, 21
Maple syrup
    Creamy Breakfast Oatmeal, 12
    Fried Grits, 69
    Maple-Cinnamon Rice Pudding, 21
    Old-Fashioned Steel-Cut Oatmeal, 15
Medium-Grain White Rice, 8
Milk
    Creamy Breakfast Oatmeal, 12
    Creamy Traditional Grits, 62
    French Polenta, 74
    Maple-Cinnamon Rice Pudding, 21
    Old-Fashioned Rice Pudding, 110
    Old-Fashioned Steel-Cut Oatmeal, 15
    Steamed Chocolate Custards, 122
    Sweet Breakfast Grits with Fresh Fruit, 22
    Tapioca Pudding, 114
    Vanilla Oatmeal Crème Brûlée with
        Berries, 16

Mint (fresh)
    Greek Lemon and Dill Rice with Feta, 30
    Rice with Fresh Greens for a Crowd, 33
Molasses, in English Pudding with
    Cranberries and Walnuts, 117

N
Napa cabbage leaves
    Steamed Halibut Steaks and Scallops with
        Sweet Red Pepper Sauce, 102–103
    Steamed Salmon Steaks with Pineapple
        Salsa, 99
Nuts
    English Pudding with Cranberries and
        Walnuts, 117
    Greek Lemon and Dill Rice with Feta, 30
    Indonesian Rice Bowl, 40–41
    Wild Rice and Bulgur with Leeks and
        Toasted Almonds, 43

O
Oatmeal
    Creamy Breakfast Oatmeal, 12
    Old-Fashioned Steel-Cut Oatmeal, 15
    Vanilla Oatmeal Crème Brûlée with
        Berries, 16
Old-Fashioned Rice Pudding, 110
Old-Fashioned Steel-Cut Oatmeal, 15
Onion(s). See also Green onions
    Basmati Rice with Corn and Peas, 37
    Butternut Squash Risotto, 88
    Frijoles Negros, 49
    Greek Lemon and Dill Rice with Feta, 30
    Herbed Green Beans, 53
    Italian White Beans, 46
    Rice Cooker Paella, 92–93
    Steamed Halibut Steaks and Scallops with
        Sweet Red Pepper Sauce, 102–103
    Steamed Salmon Steaks with Pineapple
        Salsa, 99
    Thanksgiving Jook, 26–27
On-off rice cookers, 6

P
Paella, Rice Cooker, 92–93
Parmesan cheese
    Baby Artichokes and Arborio Rice, 87
    Butternut Squash Risotto, 88
    Italian Polenta, 73
    Risotto Milanese, 91
Parsley (fresh)
    Baby Artichokes and Arborio Rice, 87
    Basmati Rice with Corn and Peas, 37
    Butternut Squash Risotto, 88
    Herbed Green Beans, 53
    Japanese White Rice with Umeboshi and
        Sesame, 34
    Rice with Fresh Greens for a Crowd, 33

Shrimp and Grits, 66–67
Steamed Shrimp and Jasmine Rice,
    104–105
Peaches, in Sweet Breakfast Grits with
    Fresh Fruit, 22
Peanuts/peanut butter, in Indonesian Rice
    Bowl, 40–41
Pears, Spiced Yams with Ginger and, 58
Peas
    Basmati Rice with Corn and Peas, 37
    Indonesian Rice Bowl, 40–41
    Rice Cooker Paella, 92–93
    Rice Pilaf with Fresh Peas, 83
Pilafs
    Bulgur and Cherry Pilaf, 80
    Lemon Basmati Pilaf, 84
    Rice Pilaf with Fresh Peas, 83
Pineapple, in Steamed Salmon Steaks with
    Pineapple Salsa, 99
Pine nuts, in Greek Lemon and Dill Rice with
    Feta, 30
Poached Rhubarb and Strawberries, 118
Polenta (yellow)
    French Polenta, 74
    Italian Polenta, 73
    Small-Portion Polenta, 77
Porridge, Rice and Sweet Potato, 25
Potatoes, in Steamed Sausages and
    Sauerkraut with Champagne, 107
Prosciutto rind, in Italian White Beans, 46
Pudding
    English Pudding with Cranberries and
        Walnuts, 117
    Tapioca Pudding, 114

R
Raisins
    Indonesian Rice Bowl, 40–41
    Maple-Cinnamon Rice Pudding, 21
Rhubarb, in Poached Rhubarb and
    Strawberries, 118
Rice and Sweet Potato Porridge, 25
Rice Cooker Paella, 92–93
Rice cookers
    cook-and-reduce-heat cooker/warmer
        type, 6
    cook-and-shut-off cooker type, 66
    fuzzy logic, 6
Rice Pilaf with Fresh Peas, 83
Rice pudding
    Maple-Cinnamon Rice Pudding, 21
    Old-Fashioned Rice Pudding, 110
    Tres Leches Rice Pudding, 113
Rice with Fresh Greens for a Crowd, 33
Riso, 8. See also Arborio rice; Carnaroli rice;
    Vialone nano rice

Risotto
  Butternut Squash Risotto, 88
  Risotto Milanese, 91
Rolled oats, in Vanilla Oatmeal Crème Brûlée
  with Berries, 16
Rosemary (fresh), in Herbed Green Beans,
  53

S
Saffron threads
  Rice Cooker Paella, 92–93
  Risotto Milanese, 91
Sake
  Steamed Ginger Salmon and Asparagus
    in Black Bean Sauce, 100
  Steamed Salmon Steaks with Pineapple
    Salsa, 99
Salmon
  Steamed Ginger Salmon and Asparagus
    in Black Bean Sauce, 100
  Steamed Salmon Steaks with Pineapple
    Salsa, 99
Salsa, in Frijoles Negros, 49
Sauerkraut, in Steamed Sausages and
    Sauerkraut with Champagne, 107
Sausage(s)
  Chinese Sausage and Rice, 38
  Rice Cooker Paella, 92–93
  Steamed Sausages and Sauerkraut with
    Champagne, 107
Scallops
  Rice Cooker Paella, 92–93
  Steamed Halibut Steaks and Scallops with
    Sweet Red Pepper Sauce, 102–103
Sesame paste (tahini), in Hummus, 50
Sesame seeds
  Chinese Sausage and Rice, 38
  Japanese White Rice with Umeboshi and
    Sesame, 34
Shallots
  Baby Artichokes and Arborio Rice, 87
  Rice Pilaf with Fresh Peas, 83
Short-Grain Brown Rice, 8
Short-grain rice. See Arborio rice
Shrimp
  Rice Cooker Paella, 92–93
  Shrimp and Grits, 66–67
  Steamed Shrimp and Jasmine Rice,
    104–105
Small-Batch Basmati Brown Rice, 8
Small-Portion Polenta, 77
Sour cream, in Steamed Halibut Steaks
    and Scallops with Sweet Red Pepper
    Sauce, 102–103
Spiced Yams with Ginger and Pears, 58
Squash, in Butternut Squash Risotto, 88
Steamed Cappuccino Custards, 121

Steamed Chicken Breasts with Warm
    Mango Sauce and Coconut Rice, 96
Steamed Chocolate Custards, 122
Steamed Corn on the Cob, 57
Steamed Ginger Salmon and Asparagus in
    Black Bean Sauce, 100
Steamed Halibut Steaks and Scallops with
    Sweet Red Pepper Sauce, 102–103
Steamed Salmon Steaks with Pineapple
    Salsa, 99
Steamed Sausages and Sauerkraut with
    Champagne, 107
Steamed Shrimp and Jasmine Rice, 104–105
Steel-cut oats
  Apple Granola, 19
  Creamy Breakfast Oatmeal, 12
  Old-Fashioned Steel-Cut Oatmeal, 15
Stone-ground grits. See Grits
Sweet Breakfast Grits with Fresh Fruit, 22
Sweetened condensed milk, in Tres Leches
    Rice Pudding, 113
Sweet potatoes
  Rice and Sweet Potato Porridge, 25
  Spiced Yams with Ginger and Pears, 58

T
Tahini, in Hummus, 50
Tapioca Pudding, 114
Texmati rice, in Rice with Fresh Greens for
    a Crowd, 33
Thai Jasmine Rice
  Indonesian Rice Bowl, 40–41
  recipe, 7
  Steamed Shrimp and Jasmine Rice,
    104–105
Thanksgiving Jook, 26–27
Thyme (fresh), in Steamed Halibut Steaks
    and Scallops with Sweet Red Pepper
    Sauce, 102–103
Tomatoes, in Rice Cooker Paella, 92–93
Tomato sauce, in Frijoles Negros, 49
Traditional Grits, 62
Tres Leches Rice Pudding, 113
Turkey, in Thanksgiving Jook, 26–27

U
Umeboshi plums, in Japanese White Rice
    with Umeboshi and Sesame, 34

V
Valencia rice, in Rice Cooker Paella, 92–93
Vanilla bean, in Poached Rhubarb and
    Strawberries, 118
Vanilla Oatmeal Crème Brûlée with Berries,
    16
Vegetable stock, in Butternut Squash
    Risotto, 88
Vialone nano rice, 8

Vialone nano rice
  Butternut Squash Risotto, 88
  Risotto Milanese, 91

W
Walnuts, in English Pudding with
    Cranberries and Walnuts, 117
Whipped cream, in Vanilla Oatmeal Crème
    Brûlée with Berries, 16
White rice. See also Arborio rice; Basmati
    rice; Jasmine rice
  American Long-Grain White Rice, 7
  Chinese Sausage and Rice, 38
  Greek Lemon and Dill Rice with Feta, 30
  Japanese White Rice with Umeboshi and
    Sesame, 34
  Lemon Basmati Pilaf, 84
  Maple-Cinnamon Rice Pudding, 21
  Medium-Grain White Rice, 8
  Rice and Sweet Potato Porridge, 25
  Rice Cooker Paella, 92–93
  Rice Pilaf with Fresh Peas, 83
  Rice with Fresh Green for a Crowd, 33
  Short-Grain White Rice, 8
  Thanksgiving Jook, 26–27
White wine
  Risotto Milanese, 91
  Steamed Chicken Breasts with Warm
    Mango Sauce and Coconut Rice, 96
  Steamed Halibut Steaks and Scallops with
    Sweet Red Pepper Sauce, 102–103
  Steamed Sausages and Sauerkraut with
    Champagne, 107
Wild Pecan Rice, 9
Wild rice, in Wild Rice and Bulgur with Leeks
    and Toasted Almonds, 43
Worcestershire sauce, in Shrimp and Grits,
    66–67

Y
Yams, in Spiced Yams with Ginger and
    Pears, 58

ALSO AVAILABLE

Air Fryer

978-0-7603-9743-5

Grilling

978-0-7603-9747-3

Smoking

978-0-7603-9745-9